MAX LAKE is among Australia's best-known writers on wine and his books have been bestsellers in Australia and well received in many other parts of the world. A Sydney surgeon, he owns a vineyard in the Hunter Valley which he named Lake's Folly. His wines bearing the Lake's Folly label have been acclaimed by wine lovers.

In October 1976 he delivered a lecture entitled 'Cabernet, the Exquisite Paradox' to the 5th Convention of the Wine and Food Society of Australia, held in the Hunter Valley. He says that 'This book is an amplification of that oration, and should further the author's quest to increase the knowledge and pleasure of those who love wine.'

CABERNET
Notes of an Australian Wineman

For Hugh Cooke

Max Lake, Sydney
November 1977

Max Lake's previous works include:
Hunter Wine
Classic Wines of Australia
Vine and Scalpel
Flavour of Wine
Hunter Winemakers

In Preparation:
Style of the Taster

Cabernet-Sauvignon: typical variety of Bordeaux; small bunches of little grapes, with hard thick skin; blue-black with whitish reflection. Makes a dark wine, charged with tannin, hard when youthful; with time develops a supple flavour, and a fine delicate bouquet of violets.

after *Dictionnaire des Vins* (48)

WINE INSTITUTE LIBRARY

CABERNET

Notes of an Australian Wineman

Max Lake

RIGBY

Gently my eyelids close
I'd rather be good than clever
and I'd rather have my facts all wrong
than have no facts whatever.

Ogden Nash

(Which is a hint to gentle readers to skip what they don't understand, in the hope of finding what they do. The book is not written for beginners although it could increase their table pleasure. The beginner should flick through this little book, wineglass in hand, at least until pleasure seduces learning. Ignore the technical stuff: most technologists will. It had to be included, if only in homage to Francis Bacon.)

Note: The figures shown in brackets in the text are references to the Bibliography.

National Library of Australia
Cataloguing-in-publication entry:

Lake, Max Emory
  Cabernet

  Index.
  Bibliography.
  ISBN 0 7270 0581 2

  1. Cabernet Sauvignon wine. I. Title

641.22

RIGBY LIMITED • ADELAIDE • SYDNEY
MELBOURNE • BRISBANE • PERTH
First published 1977
Text copyright © 1977 M. E. Lake
Illustrations copyright © 1977 Robert Ingpen
All rights reserved
Printed by Commercial Printing House Pty Ltd,
Kurralta Park, South Australia. Type set by
Modgraphic Pty Ltd, Bowden, South Australia.

Contents

APPENDICES and TABLES

Preface

Enophiles are, by definition, lovers of wine. The true enophile not only loves wines but is searching for the finest. My friend, Dr Max Lake, is such an enophile. This is the saga of his search for fine red table wines, and more specifically those primarily produced from the grape variety Cabernet Sauvignon and its cousins Cabernet franc, Malbec, Merlot and Petite Verdot.

His text centres on the history and achievements of these varieties, primarily in Australia, but he gives us a world overview of Cabernet wines, fine and otherwise.

What is a fine wine? Enophiles from Horace to Simon have shown us that quality is easily recognised. Individuals may differ in their relative appreciation of different standard wines, but it is remarkable how similarly connoisseurs react to high quality wines. For no variety is this more consistently true than for the wines of Cabernet Sauvignon.

But quality is not easily defined. Some philosophers feel that the quality of an aesthetic object, be it wine or sculpture, disappears when we try to separate its various quality parameters. I do not believe this is true and Dr Lake gives us some specific things to look for in the appearance, aroma, bouquet, after-taste and dimensions of high quality Cabernet Sauvignon wines. We can applaud his success in this.

To this we would only add that any truly great wine awes us with its aesthetic appeal. We ask ourselves, how can man make such an appealing product? A part of the attraction is that we cannot answer the question. The fabric of quality of a very fine wine is too dense and complex for complete analysis. Each sniff, each taste, even each look reveals another aspect of the quality of the wine. We never tire of it as we do of ordinary wines! And since wines change with time, each experience reveals new dimensions of colour, odour and taste, and thus of the wine's aesthetic appeal.

While all the wines of Cabernet Sauvignon belong to a common family of more or less recognisable character, individual wines from this variety differ remarkably from one another. When we add to this the extraordinary range in style and quality of its blends, we have a profound awe of the multi-dimensional potentialities of the variety.

Lake tells us of the influence of many factors: climate, crop level, time of harvest, method of crushing, fermenting and aging, etc. But over and above these factors are the unknown, subtle or unrecognised technological influences on quality. The microflora of the vineyard and the winery, the yeast cultures used, the time of racking, the cleanliness of the cooperage, the type and size of cooperage and the winemakers' decisions of which wines to include or exclude from the blends are also important. Why should Chateau 'X' 1966 be so different from its nearby 1966 sisters? The subtle alchemistry of grape-grower and enologist results in an aesthetic achievement that is greater than either. How they do it, neither they nor we understand.

Not all the wines of this variety are great. No-one, not even Dr Lake, would claim they were. I, for one, have a healthy scepticism as to claims for the quality of some of the legendary wines of this variety of the last and this century. In their optimum time they may have been fine and even great. But it is the wine in the glass, not its label or age, which counts.

Welcome then to the wonderful world of the red wines of Cabernet Sauvignon. And thank Dr Lake for his perceptive introduction to one of the most complex and amazing wines man has yet created.

Maynard A. Amerine

Acknowledgments

Warmest thanks once again to Professor Maynard Amerine for the preface; for criticism gratefully received, if not always acted on; wide knowledge, fine palate, references; and general support so generously given.

Dr John Austwick, Peter Bailey, John Beeston, Robin Bradley, John Elliot, Claude Corne, Lydia Crawford, Doug and Judy Crittenden, Brian Croser, Ross Drewitt, Victor Gibson, Dr Grant Dickson, Graham Gregory, David Hardy, Ian Hickinbotham, Dick Heath, Roland Hill, Mark Hill-Smith, Peter Joyce, George Kerridge, Chess Krawczyk, Dr John Middleton, Ian Nott, D. K. W. Perry, James Quinlan, Dr Bryce Rankine, Rupert Rosenblum, Jack Shipton, Dr Lou Skinner, Dr Chris Somers, John Stanford, John Thorp, and Frank Thorpy have all helped in many ways.

Lucky is the author with the aid of a wife like Joy and a secretary like Colleen Barden.

The Estate of the late Ogden Nash gave permission for use of the quotation from that author, and Jonathan Cape Limited for the quotation from Kurt Vonnegut Jr.

Max Lake
Sydney
1977

CHAPTER ONE

The exquisite paradox

Cabernet Sauvignon is an extraordinary offering to the winelover of sensitivity, whether plain enjoyer or connoisseur. Philosophers might debate, goblets in hand, how much of the greatness of the world's red wines is vested in the dusted blue globular berries of this variety. There are nineteen species of grape vines in Asia and the Americas, but only one native to Europe, *Vitis vinifera*, whose members, remarkably, make all the great wines in the world. Cabernet Sauvignon, to many, is the supreme vinifera (52). It makes *the* wine for an occasion.

Pinotphiles, secretly or otherwise, enjoy the bottle-aged virtues of Cabernet: particularly from those regions where the volume of flavour and balance of the wines of the two varieties at their best approach each other in mellow maturity.

For the fullest flowering of his art, each artist chooses his preferred medium. The composer might select voice. A cabinetmaker could favour cedar. The painter who works on canvas achieves a unique texture. A potter may venture into porcelain, with all its inherent difficulties because he can achieve a delicacy of form, and nuance of glaze, that glorify his art. In winemaking, the winemaker may select Cabernet Sauvignon because it gives a wine without parallel in the elegance of its maturity.

Yet few natural gifts display more paradoxes. The exquisite complexity of flavour that may be derived from this single fruit is hard to match. How striking it is that among thousands of different grapes, only two or three others compare in the intensity of their specific character. Such flavour tends to generosity, but can be meagre.

The Cabernet Sauvignon vine grows with extraordinary vigour in the right conditions, yet its production of fruit is quite restrained until the vigneron learns to match his wits against this natural tendency. Despite its shyness about reproduction, it is very adaptable. The number of vines planted per acre, whether 500 or 2,000, have less influence upon flavour than the location of the vineyard and the method of growing the vine.

A vine dresser needs surgical skill to persuade the vine to fruit adequately, and he needs the resilience of spring steel to prune the wiry canes day after day in the winter cold. It is surely hardest of all varieties.

The paradoxes increase. Picking needs frequent resharpening of knife, good secateurs, or a hacksaw blade. Yet, under the assault of the epileptiform mechanical harvester, the ripe fruit falls off the bunches with great ease.

Not only is the vine a relatively poor cropper, as befits such an aristocrat (it yields only half the production of Hermitage), but the small grape has a low volume of free run wine from a high ratio of skin and pips to grape size. It also has less, and heavier, presswine. It tends to reach optimum maturity just after mid-season, which leads into the cooler autumn ripening period. This rather enhances the best development of colour and flavour. Serendipity!

Few grapes give better rewards to the grower in poor years. It has a buffer capacity, to withstand climatic or winemaking insult, that can only be described as infinitely forgiving. Some of the good Cabernet wines, for example Bordeaux' Latour and the Hunter's Lake's Folly, come from 'off years'. The thick skin improves its resistance to rain. Even in the Hunter Valley, a very presentable wine can often be made in a wet year. This point certainly was proved in the disastrously wet 1971 vintage. The winegrowers there, who scoffed when I based the Folly on Cabernet Sauvignon, became silent that year.

The young wine, even free run, may be acid and hard, with years to soften before it is pleasant, but it is invariably worth the wait.

In the 1940s no labelled Australian Cabernets were easily available simply because there was not much Cabernet grown. Probably the principal reason for the increase in Cabernet wines is the fact that there are so many recently educated palates who are prepared to pay for the privilege of drinking top wines, produced at a cost well above that of the dependable Shiraz Hermitage in Australia at least. Only in the last few decades has the consumer understood what the grower has known since the first half of last century: that Cabernet Sauvignon is a difficult child, but a splendiferous adult.

No one really knows where Cabernet comes from. Until recent memory, those

10

growing it were not likely to keep careful data. The first record of grape names, kept in Bordeaux, dates from the sixteenth century, but all the Cabernet vines in the world today stem from a single cane or seed planted before recorded history. Nobody has ever succeeded in breeding it true from seed since it became known. Only by planting the cuttings from a vine, or grafting a bud from a vine to another stock, has Cabernet, as we know it, survived. Occasional spontaneous development of sports (of the vines!) further confuse the canvas. Despite this, there does seem to be a pattern which allows us to make fairly reasonable deductions.

Fossils show that wild vines existed in pre-history. As far as the connoisseurs of Egypt and Babylon are concerned, it is difficult enough today to differentiate between the wine made from grapes or dates, let alone between grape varieties. In Roman times, when both Pliny and Columella discussed the wines of Bordeaux, the tribe living in the Bordeaux area was the Bituriges and the grape variety they cultivated was the Biturica, but whether this name derived from Columella's abbreviation, or from *Vitis dura* (hard vine) is lost now. The name is not a bad description, for, as Columella says, the vine stood cold better than damp, damp better than drought, and 'bore up cheerfully against heat'. Ausonius, the Bordeaux-born poet, professor, and Governor of Gaul in the fourth century, had vineyards at Pauillac, and possibly at Chateau Ausone.

The Romans may well have fostered the propagation of such a variety, to withstand the rigours of a more northern climate. Grape-growing was certainly under strict government control throughout the whole Roman Empire, both as to quantity and variety. 'A hard finish to the wine and six years old before it was fit to drink,' does sound like our modern Cabernet Sauvignon (55).

Isidor reported from Seville early in the seventh century that the variety Biturique 'takes its name from the country where it is cultivated, resistant to wind, rain and heat, and does well in poor ground, and is thus more important than other varieties'. In the fifteenth century, pale or 'rose' wine made from red grapes, clear and light coloured from being taken quickly off the skins, was called *vin clairet*. Clairet had also become a term for the wines of Orleans, 'recommended for those who were faint after too much use of women'. (Maison Rustique.) The English soon anglicised the word into 'claret' (83).

It is interesting that about this time winemaking without stalks began both in Italy and France, but was not general practice in Bordeaux or Australia until the present century.

In 1152, Henry Plantagenet of England married Eleanor of Aquitaine, the ancient province of south-west France which included Bordeaux. He became Henry II of England in 1154. For the next three hundred years, a period in which England dominated a large part of France, the wine of Bordeaux was sold in

Britain as an English product. In fact André Simon points out that the wines usually travelled more easily to London than to the rest of France, perhaps because sea transport was swifter than land travel in those days. Those who have travelled the area will realise that the Bordelais still speak French with the English nasal twang. General Talbot (after whom one of my favourite Bordeaux is named) was killed in the battle of Castillon in 1453 when Bordeaux became French again (65).

For centuries, claret was a favourite wine of the middle and upper classes of England and Scotland. On 18 February 1819, John Keats wrote to his brother and sister-in-law George and Georgina in America that 'I like claret . . . For really 'tis so fine it fills one's mouth with a gushing freshness — then goes down cool and feverless — then you do not feel it quarrelling with your liver — no, it is rather a Peacemaker, and lies as quiet as it did in the grape; then it is as fragrant as the Queen Bee, and the more ethereal part of it mounts into the Brain, not assaulting the cerebral apartments like a bully in a badhouse looking for his trull, and hurrying from door to door bouncing against the wainscot, but rather walks like Aladdin about his enchanted palace so gently that you do not feel his step.'

Knowledge of claret was part of the education of a British gentleman, and during the great years of foundation of the British Empire they took this knowledge with them to the 'colonies'. Dr Alexander Kelly (40) quotes Monsieur d'Armailhacq.

Petit-Lafitte quoting a 1784 catalogue, gives details of contemporary Cabernets. There were two main varieties: Cabernet Sauvignon and Cabernet Gros, and an excess of sub-varieties. In those days, Cabernet Sauvignon included Cabernelle, Carmenère, Petit-Cabernet-Sauvignon, Petit Bouschet, and Vidure. At Libourne it was called, aptly enough, Petit Fer (little iron: a reference to its hard finish). Nowadays, the variety Cabernelle, Carmenère, or Grand Vidure is regarded as a third variety of Cabernet, after Cabernet Sauvignon and Cabernet franc (76).

Cabernet Gros included Cabernet franc, Gros Cabernet-Sauvignon, Carmenet, and Grosse Vigne dure. In Vienne it was called Bretton; in Saumur it was Veronais; and in the Pyrenees it was Arrouya. St-Emilion still calls it Bouchet, classed as true Cabernet franc.

'I could not live without your words, no matter how you spell them.'

(Mathews.)

There are literally dozens of synonyms. Later, there are so many spellings when we trace the vine around Australia, that if we leave the letters C, N, and T of Cabernet in fixed positions enough letters of the alphabet could be juggled in between them to delight the most undisciplined 'Scrabble' player. They include Carbenet Savignien of Hobart Botanic Garden, 1857 (58).

Bordeaux classification started in 1647, followed by another in 1767 after vast plantings at the beginning of that century. Further classifications followed. While these imply a change in fortunes for individual vineyards, there is also evident a continuous upgrading of style and quality. This culminated in the strict limitation of production and the removal of all but six declared varieties of vines: Cabernet Sauvignon, Cabernet franc, Carmenère, Merlot, Malbec, and Petit Verdot.

By the second half of last century, Cabernet Sauvignon had been planted in many parts of the world. James Busby, the pioneer viticulturist, brought cuttings to Australia among his collection of vine cuttings from Europe, and the vine was established in the Sydney Botanic Garden.

In Busby's first catalogue (18), Number 55 is *Carbenet or C. à Petits Grains* — de la Gironde. 'This variety and the three following, are almost exclusively cultivated in the vineyards of the Médoc and the *Carbenet à Petits Grains* and *Carbenet Sauvignen* (sic) are alone to be found in those of highest reputation.' The cuttings were from the nursery of the Luxembourg in Paris.

Suttor (71) described the Claret-grape of Margaux, and the Carmenet, as the best wine grapes.

Bleasdale (10–13) gives details, varieties, vineyards, strengths, and growers, of both straight Cabernets and blends of wines, from Victoria, South Australia, and New South Wales. In his last paper, referring to the great red wines of South Australia, he advised 'Carbinet, and blends of it for the highlands; Shiraz including Hermitage, and Mataro and blends of it, generally everywhere. For persons having an established relish for wines of the kind we call French clarets, blends of Carbinet with a wine of more natural body, such as Shiraz, will always be favourite.' Pettavel (56) does not list Cabernet among 'the kinds of wine . . . proved to be the most successful in the Colony [Victoria].' This situation was rapidly corrected by the urgings of Guyot (1865 Melbourne translation) who was particularly impressed with the dominance of Cabernet character. 'If Chateau Lafitte was planted with Gamais, it would produce a very inferior wine. But if the Cabernet Sauvignon of Médoc . . . was cultivated at Madeira, at the Cape, in Spain, in Algeria, or Auxerre, in each locality they would produce good wines which would remind one of the best Bordeaux . . . the cepages kept by wealthy and intelligent men have remained almost an object of worship.'

Dr Alexander Kelly wrote in 1861 that 'Cabernet Sauvignon is said to bear well in New South Wales, but is unsuited to this Colony [South Australia] except perhaps in colder districts. It is known by various names in France, and there seem to be two varieties cultivated there. It is difficult to say which of the two we have in this Colony.' The Cabernet he planted still grows below the ridge at Tintara, near McLaren Vale.

Several Cabernets and clarets (variety unspecified) from the Hunter Valley and Albury are in the official catalogue of wines from New South Wales shown at the Bordeaux exhibition of 1882. At a Vienna exhibition of the same period, the judges rejected Australian entries because they believed that wines of such superior quality must be French (78).

Francois de Couesland conducted the 1877 vintage at Tahbilk, with Cabernet among about ten other varieties. The Purbricks, who over the past half-century have raised the vineyard to its present high place, until recently labelled their Cabernets with the accessory description BURGUNDY, because Eric Purbrick was impressed by the size of the wine from Tahbilk soil and climate. Varietal nomenclature has since consigned such descriptions to history.

The Army and Navy Stores (London) catalogue of 1870 features a compendious wine list, including a Dalwood Cabernet at a high price. Audrey Wilkinson was the last to market a Cabernet as such from the lower Hunter Valley until the author was influenced to start a Cabernet vineyard by tasting a 1930 'Hunter River Cabernet' *chez* Crittenden, the best red in my experience up to 1960. (See illustration on jacket.) Of an extraordinarily complex flavour, it was a supple and elegant wine consisting of equal parts Cabernet Sauvignon and Petit Verdot, grown at Dalwood. Only three hogsheads were made, and the vines were pulled out!

The fortunes of Cabernet in Australia declined steadily after phylloxera ravaged the Victorian vineyards in the 1890s and the bank crash of the same period ruined a number of vignerons. The number of connoisseurs decreased, and the Australian wine world was affected by matters as diverse as the 1930s depression, the second World War, and vine diseases like black spot and downy mildew.

Cabernet existed at Coonawarra for a long period, though in small quantities, since 1891 (8) (31). Jack Mann of Houghton's, in Western Australia's Swan Valley, started labelling some of his reds Cabernet after the second World War, as did Sandalford. These vines came from South Africa last century, and are the source of the high-bearing clone number 11 of the Western Australian Department of Agriculture. Penfold's had private bin Cabernet labels in the 1940s, from Kalimna for example. Some readers will have partaken of the tiny quantity of the fabulous 1952 Grange Cabernet and the lesser and more controversial 1959 and others. Hardy's were also labelling Cabernet in this period; some from Coonawarra, and some from McLaren Vale. The first Seven Hills Cabernet dry red wine that I tasted was the 1954, although there has been information of a 1953. Seppelt's labelled Cabernet (from Barossa material) from 1950 and 1951 and probably even earlier.

Some wine exhibitions have included a 'sparkling red burgundy' class, dominated by Seppelt's Cabernet styles. Even when these red ancients gave up the ghost and ceased bubbling, they remained redolent of cigar box and cedar, and were superb to drink as still wines.

Most of the principal 'clarets' or varietally-labelled Cabernet blends which are now household names, started in the 1950s. In Australia, there was no systematic use of new oak cooperage for red wines before that period. The effects of its introduction, by such winemakers as John Davoren, Colin Preece, and Max Schubert, diffused throughout the industry. It is paradoxical that the quasi-Bordeaux style, now established as Penfold's top red, is based on the Shiraz variety of grape, although the first experiments and several subsequent wines involved Cabernet. This may indicate that there was little acceptance of Cabernet Sauvignon in Australia as recently as twenty years ago.

In 1950, the only Cabernet wines produced commercially came from Reynella, apart from a few truly private bins bottled by Hardy's, Penfold's, Seppelt's, Tahbilk, and Bill Redman's wines distributed by other companies. Also there were a few historical marvels from Sunbury, Clare, Whittlesea, other Port Phillip/Yarra vineyards, Pokolbin and Dalwood, but the entire production represented only a drop in the ocean (or rather pond) of Australian wine consumption of that time.

In 1967 (14), the time of the only recent published Australian attempt at grape classification, Cabernet Sauvignon in South Australia totalled 700 acres, of which about 100 were irrigated. Now there are 10,000 acres in Australia, of which more than half are in South Australia. The total production of Cabernet wine is more than 3 million gallons per annum. The jump in the last two decades is remarkable, e.g. two to more than thirty vineyards growing Cabernet in the lower Hunter, in less than ten years, and a twelve times increase of production in the past five years.

The sustained quality of irrigation area wines, with fairly high volumes of wine produced per acre, is part of this movement. The high volume production and quality of the 'self irrigating' Coonawarras is to be expected because of the miraculous soil profile, but irrigation area Cabernet of the quality of McWilliams and Berri, to name but two, have been a continuing pleasure to palate and pocket. Now there are more than 100 Cabernet labels in Australia, and at least twenty per cent more producers here than in California.

The author's missions into the field of wine (42–47) prompted, simply enough, by admiration for what wine is and does, have been a part of an era in which the winegrowing industry has known increasing success. It reflects a general upward social mobility and an improvement in the community palate.

One development of the Australian wine boom of the late 1960s which should be recorded for posterity was the move into the local industry by multi-national corporations. The two best value-for-money Cabernets of the period were Stanley's Clare Leasingham and Orlando's Barossa, made by the two wineries who were among the first to fall to the invaders. It is a pleasure to record that the invasion has not caused any loss of quality, and of course there is no reason why quality should have deteriorated, at least in Australia. This has not always been the case with Australian wine sold in England, by the English boards of Australian firms. On the other side of the coin I had the slightly chauvinistic pleasure of tasting, on a 1972 visit to the heart of California's wineland, a Cabernet Sauvignon made by Kaiser Stuhl, the great Barossa Valley Cooperative, which competed favourably with Californian wines both in quality and price.

There are three primary strata of winegrowers now in Australia: big, medium and small. Excellent Cabernet wines are obtainable on all levels, either the peak of a carefully handled segment of one of the larger operations or virtually the whole production of small specialist vineyards, with graduations in between. All have wood character (flavour and maturation) added by the winemaker, according to his art.

Many consumers still prefer reds of other varieties, particularly where price is the dominant consideration. However, as in all walks of life, as this century draws on, and technology enhances technique, the enjoyer will seek ever more ardently for the best he can afford. In wine, Cabernet will rank high.

CHAPTER TWO

The grape

One hundred and fifty
days and nights;
rain and hail,
zephyr and gale;
bugs and birds,
sun blaze,
then quiet dark—
ambrosia.

The baby leaves of Cabernet Sauvignon shoot from furry little buds a month or so after Spring starts. About a hundred and fifty days later, the grapes are fermenting in the winery.

As the leaves grow to maturity, they are shiny, deep green, small to medium size, with toothed edges more definitely serrated than most other varieties. Each leaf has five lobes, with long sharp points. Many of these overlap near the base and give the leaf an appearance of perforation. As you work along the vine rows it takes little imagination to sense the gaze of the little 'eyes' in the leaves; friendly, if reserved.

The canes are reddish when they are young and they turn a deep brown at maturity. Healthy bunches of grapes, of medium size, attach to the cane by a wiry stalk which turns brown when they are ripe. The bunches are long and cylindrical, or tending to a cone shape. Occasionally there is a projection at the top, but nothing like the large truly conical bunch of Shiraz/Hermitage with its frequently generous boobs.

The berries are small and quite round. They have a thick tough skin containing a high volume of seeds and viscid pulp matter, rather sticky when ripe. One needs a good part of a bunch to get a mouthful of juice, a wasteful vintage pleasure. Apart from the easy recognition of the variety by the 'eyes' in the leaf, the most striking thing about ripe Cabernet Sauvignon grapes is their deep violet-blue colour, with a whitish bloom of wax and probably yeasts, on well-kept vines. The relevance of this bloom, to flavour, will be considered later.

Many growers of Cabernet Sauvignon wines think that they tend to produce better in alternate years, but this could be related simply to pruning techniques.

Cabernet Sauvignon will do well anywhere in the world where sun, soil, and drainage are suitable for the growth of *vitis* varieties. The most remarkable thing about the wine is its ability to reproduce a dominant varietal quality in its wine wherever it is grown. This certainly does not apply to Pinot Noir, its competitor for our affections. The similarities of the top Cabernets, for example in Australia, California, Chile and Bulgaria, to those of Bordeaux straight Cabernet, are much more obvious than the differences. Of course the two different flavour profiles, described later, may be found within these countries, but always dependent upon good winemaking of whatever style, stamped by varietal character and development. Paradoxically, there can be as much variation in Cabernet style within a limited area as you may find between the Cabernets of the countries mentioned.

Amerine and Joslyn (2) state 'California Cabernet is a distinctive type of wine which is produced from at least 51 per cent of the Cabernet Sauvignon variety and has the predominant aroma and flavour of that grape. It is a moderately well-coloured wine of good extract and alcohol. The better Cabernet wines are heavy-bodied, have a full ruby-red colour, and a total acidity of not less than 0.60 per cent.' The Wine Institute specification for Cabernet is: 'A dry red table wine produced of Cabernet Sauvignon Grapes. In this type the heavier-bodied and darker coloured wines should be on an equal basis with the lighter-bodied and lighter-coloured wines. It should be well balanced and aged, both in wood and bottle. It should have a distinctive bottle bouquet.' California Cabernet is likely to be of lesser quality than California Cabernet Sauvignon.

Micro-climate has a marked influence on acidity, and alcohol.

Winkler regards California climatic regions 2 and 3 (based on heat summation as degree days) as ideal for Cabernet Sauvignon but quite obviously the vine does well in special parts of 1 and 4. (See Appendices V, VII, and VIII.)

The last word has not been spoken on the influence of local and general climate on the quality of Cabernet Sauvignon. It seems now that even more important than degree-days may be temperature curves and solar radiation (Prescott, quoted by Elliott). This would explain why an area like the lower Hunter Valley which is basically sub-tropical produces such outstanding wines; Hickinbotham suggested this is a factor of its fairly constant cloud cover. Concrete evidence of the effect of climate is seen in Appendices V, VII, and VIII.

On the subject of the best soil for Cabernet grapes, some consider the requirements are simply good drainage, low to moderate fertility, and an ordinary balance of minerals. The varietal dominance will do the rest, unless parasites indicate root-stock or other prophylaxis. You will find a lot more than this in some wine books (20).

Traditional propagation, by cutting canes, from one vine to a new planting, has ensured the survival and a degree of uniformity of Cabernet Sauvignon. Differences within this variety occur from mutation, perhaps by the influence of cosmic rays, of virus and other diseases, and unknown factors. In my own vineyard, on one vine during a particular season, may occasionally be observed a quite different leaf, or bunch form, on one cane, than on the rest of that single vine. Cuttings taken from that branch probably would produce a different 'Cabernet Sauvignon'. This starts to explain some of the varietal variation seen.

Propagation by the sexual production (it had to rear its head sooner or later) and planting of seed, either intra- or cross-varietal, results in offspring which share Cabernet Sauvignon character but not necessarily in a dominant way. The famous Ruby Cabernet of California is one of these, from Cabernet Sauvignon and Carignan, producing a wine of some Cabernet complexity in the nose, quite good colour and a more generous production per vine. This and the numerous other Cabernets, have not displaced the original Cabernet Sauvignon as the 'back-bone of an elegant claret (54)'. What has happened however, by careful clonal selection in the past twenty years, is that the production of high quality grapes per vine has, in some instances, been doubled. This may not have been a positive contribution to flavour, as discussed later.

Apart from the Busby collection, and Silesian importations to South Australia, there have been others, including those of the CSIRO, and some of the large private firms, who can bear the expense of quarantine, in a continuing search for improvement. I believe the grape itself is infrequently the cause of reduced *quality* whatever the clone; the West Australian Department of Agriculture's selection program for quantity, as well as quality, production has been most successful.

One authority recently stated 'history will show that the Cabernet Sauvignon we have had to grow in this country [Australia] in the past, has only ever yielded mediocre wine'. Here are the views of three who were overlooked in that comment. Take David Sutherland Smith (70) on *Outstanding Australian Wines*. 'The other amazing claret is Dawson's, of Whittlesea—vintage 1929—some of you may remember this wine. For many years I did not know whether it was Dawson's 1929 or La Fite 1929—I was never sure. The last bottle I tasted was at one of our Viticultural luncheons last year. On that day we had the French Consul as our guest. The labels were, as usual, covered, and of course he called Dawson's claret a first growth French wine. The other red wine that went around with it happened to be a Chateau Margaux 1934, the high rating of 6 points. Our French friend's description of it was "A very good Australian wine—nothing to be ashamed of really"'.

'Perhaps by sheer luck I was able to recognise both wines before the wrapper was removed and I entered into a verbal battle with our guest. In my most polite and dignified manner I contradicted him. Our French Consul took it all in good part, especially after being so dogmatic, but after lunch he told me I was the best judge he had met in Australia; I did not let on it was really a memory test. I think Tom Seabrook, knowing the French Consul was coming, deliberately provided us with the best Australian and the best French clarets. We all agreed with the Consul that Dawson's Claret was the better wine. This claret was made from Cabernet Sauvignon with some Malbec; it was like a typical French claret in every respect.'

T. C. Seabrook stated in 1948 'I assert with some authority that most comparisons of French and Australian wines have been made on a manifestly unfair basis. In the first place, many of the French wines are classified growths with full maturity—the epitome of quality, and not representative of the average wine of France, whereas the Australian reds that come into comparison are often drawn from commercial sources, where expediency demands that not too much time should be devoted to acquiring bottle age.

'Secondly, I have proved beyond doubt that this quick turnover has robbed these wines of any possibility of coming into their own. Time and time again I have seen "left-overs" from bins years after the wines ceased to have any commercial significance and the development has been astounding. It should be a routine practice for every bottler of a promising wine to rigidly segregate at least a gross for a minimum of ten years, then release it to those capable of proper appreciation. I venture to say that such wines would bring Australian and French comparisons into much better and logical perspective.

'Contrariwise, the wines now arriving in Australia from the Continent are much younger than pre-war, so much so as to justify a comment recently made: "The nearest approach to an Australian wine of any French wine yet tasted."

'Recently I had the opportunity of contrasting two very old wines dug up out of a dis-used wine cellar, having similar characteristics, except that the first tasted was decrepit and finished, whilst the second was still vigorous and drinkable. The first turned out to be Chateau Malescot St Exupéry and the second Chateau Yering Cabernet Sauvignon, from Lilydale, Victoria, a wine very famous in its time but surprising to encounter today. Besides being the better wine, it was more French in its style than the Third Growth Chateau Malescot.

'Other fine reds of my acquaintance which showed pronounced French style were those of R. E. Dawson of Whittlesea—especially 1929 vintage—some old Geelong wines from Pilloud's vineyard, 1928 Cabernet and Hermitage from H. D. Young of Kanmantoo, others from W. H. Gillard of Clarendon, South Australia, 1932 and 1935 vintages from Woodley Wines Limited, 1933 vintage of Reynella, 1936 Burgundy from Peter Pola of Great Western and many others too numerous to mention.'

In a paper read at a meeting of the Royal Colonial Institute, London, in 1888, Hubert de Castella of Yering described the result of a Tasting held in Melbourne earlier. 'The participants at the Tasting, mostly vineyard proprietors themselves, were augmented by a few professional men; all were winelovers, and all considered themselves knowledgeable. The trial of Red wines included a Chateau Lafite, priced at 90/- per dozen, a Chateau Latour from the Melbourne Club, three or four Bordeaux from London, and almost a dozen of the Vignerons' own wines, to which one of the guests of the evening had added a bottle of old wine grown at Yering on the Yarra. When wrapped samples were gone through, an exchange of opinions was permitted. Great excitement prevailed. One of the wines was awarded the highest marks by almost every Taster. When the Secretary began systematically with No. 1, reporting the points recorded, no one paid any attention. "Take No. 8 first," they all exclaimed. "What is No. 8?" Giving way to impatience, and removing the paper covering, the Secretary rose, himself excited, and read the name of a Victorian, the grower of the Yering wine.'

Colin Preece (59) continues: 'Some compassion may perhaps be felt for the fatuity of an Australian who speaks of Australian wines in the same breath as Chateau Lafite. With the fear that what I have seen so often may be considered the outcome of prejudice, I qualify by saying that had judges trained especially with Bordeaux wines of stereotyped and almost conventional flavours, been invited to classify the wines, they would have perhaps recognised, I will not say the classic wines but the type of classic wines, and reverently placed them above all others. But the jury was composed, as is invariably the case, of an assemblage of men not influenced by mere labels, who classified as best the wine which with equal cleanness and delicacy, struck them most by the brilliancy of its other qualities.'

As Mamet wrote:

If a duckling could say 'What a beautiful day'
he wouldn't mean sunny and fair
'cause a duck looks at things in a different way
he would mean it was wet everywhere.

These quotations from older and more experienced palates make it difficult to keep silent. Caution is taught by the facts that (a) some Bordeaux reds of certain years are so exquisitely complex as to totally ravish the senses; and (b) the author is a Cabernet winemaker to whom the sometime comparison of his own wines with great Cabernets elsewhere tends to overbalance self-criticism, but it does seem that the 1,000-year advantage enjoyed by the French winemakers has lessened considerably.

The Californians, frequently circumspect in their oenochauvinism, finally broke bounds recently, as Moira Johnston exultantly described it in *The Year California Won the Pennant*. (See Appendix III.) The French did not take this very calmly. Odette Kahn's reply (38) was even subtitled: 'On the subject of a "small scandal", an unconvincing editorial apologia.

Absolute comparison of national and regional styles of Cabernet wines is extraordinarily difficult. Bacon could well have asked 'What is truth?' There are no absolute palates. Nonetheless winelovers are going increasingly to amuse and instruct themselves and their friends with such exercises. There will be peaks of Australian, Californian, French and the rest, the best that can be done with the magnificent Cabernet grape of *that* season, from *that* vineyard, by *that* winemaker. Why not?

No offering on Cabernet Sauvignon would be complete without reference to the characteristics of its brothers, sisters, and cousins. Last century d'Armailhacq wrote about Cabernet Gros or Carmenet. He described five varieties, the white Cabernet, the natur or grey Cabernet, the late Cabernet, the red Cabernet and the Cabernet of St John. These days vignerons tend to refer to Cabernet franc, but it is obvious there are many Sauvignon mutations around. What does distinguish them from the monarch is that their canes are less red and brown than Sauvignon, the leaves tend to be less downy, and the 'eyes' less obvious. The wines mature quicker and tend to have less tannin, with slightly less colour and complexity of flavour. At full time maturity it may bear less than Sauvignon (Amerine, Pers. comm.). It may be more commonly grown in Bordeaux than is realised.

Merlot is quite uncommon in Australia, but this grape is considered by some students to give the great Bordeaux much of their richness and suppleness of flavour on the middle of the palate, particularly in view of its consistently lower malic acid compared to Cabernet (57). The Australian Merlot wines I have tasted do not, yet, follow this view. The leaf has three lobes, separated by an interval. The teeth on the edge of the leaf are more projecting and the size in general larger than the Cabernet leaf. The bunch is long and rather branched and while the berries have a blue-blackish colour and floury bloom similar to Cabernet, the seeds are much smaller. The canes are paler also.

Malbec has been a much more successful variety in Australia and some of the straight Malbec wines (Angle Vale, Berri Co-op., Best's Great Western, Hamilton's, Houghton, Kaiser Stuhl, Leasingham, Milawa, Penfold's, St Clare, and Seppelt's) made here have been good to superb. Malbec does seem to have played some part in filling the middle palate of those wines of the austere Cabernet Sauvignon style (see later). D'Armailhacq stated the best distinguishing feature of the grape is the bright red stalk when the bunch is ripe. The leaves are thicker than the Cabernet and of a duller colour, with an early rather 'cottony and downy' appearance early in the season. The three rounded lobes have much less prominent teeth on the edges. The leaf may appear to be quite round. The grapes are bigger than Cabernet Sauvignon and less tightly packed in the bunch. The bunch itself is squatter; sometimes almost triangular.

These varieties have all been used in various proportions in Bordeaux winemaking. (See Table 3A.)

The final and definitive comment on the effects of climate is made of course in vintage tables. The real connoisseur knows how to read between the lines of these tables, but they do give some indication of what the general conditions were like in a particular district in one year.

Influences other than effective climate have a considerable effect on grape quality. They are pruning practice, fertiliser, and irrigation.

It is interesting to note the conditions of the 1965 Control of Appellation Permit, which lays down the legal requirement for vignerons who wish to use a specific 'appellation', or label, on French wines. This limits the appellation to thirty hectolitres of wine per acre for a commune listing, forty-three for Haut-Médoc, and forty-five for Médoc. In terms of imperial gallons per acre I came up with a set of figures for the old First Growths, based on data available at the time: Mouton-Rothschild 100 gallons per acre, Haut-Brion 143, Latour 200, Lafite 223 and Margaux 266.

CHAPTER THREE

The flavour of cabernet wine

'Oh, the vanity of wine tasting!'
(Defence attorney at the fraud trial
of Bordeaux négociants; 1974).

What of the pedants? Larousse says the Cabernet Sauvignon grape makes 'a dark wine charged with tannin, hard when youthful but with time develops a body of subtleness and a fine and delicate bouquet of violets'; and of Cabernet franc that it has 'less perfume, but ages quicker'. Feret (29) is worth quoting. 'The wine is brilliant and vivid in colour, hard when first made, but acquiring, as it ages, a mellow delicate flavour and a sweet and abundant perfume, more defined than those of other wines. It takes a long time in developing and becoming agreeable, but it ages for a considerable time, gaining in quality.'

Dr Kelly wrote 'The wine made from Cabernet Sauvignon is very delicate. It has a peculiar flavour and a great deal of bouquet and perfume. Its colour is good, and deeper than that of Cabernet Gros. In some very dry years, the skin of this grape becomes a little hard and would give roughness to the wine if too much pressed. It is this which has determined several proprietors to make wine without crushing the grape and to take out the stalks. This wine keeps a great length of time and its keeping qualities are as great or greater than those of the wine made from the Cabernet Gros. It requires generally one year or more of the cask before being bottled.'

A hundred years later Penning Rowsell (54) stated 'It is the Cabernet Sauvignon which produces much of the deep colour, the "bloom" of the aroma, the finesse and the "cut" in the flavour of a fine Médoc; the "backbone" of an elegant claret.'

Dr Chris Somers describes three landmarks to the recognition of Cabernet Sauvignon: deep colour; the characteristic grape smell of fresh blackcurrants or cedar; and length of flavour in combination with tannin and acidity. These may all vary somewhat in strength, not only because of differences of soil and micro-climate but also because Cabernet Sauvignon grapes are usually blended with others in winemaking. Before elaborating on the odour and flavour of Cabernet Sauvignon, one should differentiate clearly between the fruit *aroma* of young wine on the one hand, and the *bouquet* of the mature wine on the other. Webb's (79) classification of influences dictating wine flavour helps to clarify the point. He lists (1) Raw fruit flavour (2) ditto altered during fermentation (3) Action of yeasts (4) Cellar operations (5) Aging.

Each of these is quite different, but all except the first depend upon the fact that maturity of wine is really a very slow and controlled oxidation.

The newly fermented wine of Cabernet Sauvignon grapes has several characteristic odour tones, wherever it is grown. Possibly the most characteristic and common, is a greenish character, which may well be compared to that of freshly mown herbage. (Pinot-reared Burgundian baroness, asked for her opinion on a young Cabernet, replied 'Ah, but I would not drink green grass!') This may be the precursor of a later suggestion of mint. Some people call it a 'stalky' character, describing more the smell than the taste: I prefer to avoid this description because it appears in Cabernet wine which has had no contact with stalks. 'Stalky' should be kept for stalky flavours, particularly a hardness of the kind easily tasted by sucking a grape stalk.

The basic fruit odour of the young wine is close enough to blackcurrant, though occasionally it recalls other berry fruits such as mulberry, elderberry flowers, or, more rarely, blackberry. A rich Shiraz sometimes has a blackberry character, which may trap one into thinking that it is a Cabernet. Amerine and co-authors define the varietal aroma of Californian Cabernet as 'musty, aromatic'. Early in the development of the wine, the ravishing odour of truffle may be easily nosed in some wines. (Everyone ought to indulge himself in a genuine truffle once in his life; at least from a can, if you don't have a trained pig or dog to root one up in traditional style.) In Australian Cabernets this can mingle with a 'dusty' note, which is probably the Californian 'musty'. An occasional hint of resin (eucalypt in Australia, redwood in California, pine in Bordeaux and Coonawarra) may be due to volatile oils from those trees becoming fixed by the whitish bloom wax of the ripe grapes.

The mature wine of Cabernet Sauvignon is quite different. The characteristic aroma described above has passed. Now one might pick up a scent resembling cedar oil or a fine cigar box. Less commonly, there is a lovely delicate floral tone which the poetic see as violets. Frequently there is more than a hint of mint, inclining towards the spiciness, though not the pungency, of fresh-ground pepper, or sometimes just common or garden mint. If there was any almond character in the young wine, it may persevere into maturity. (The stalks of ripe Cabernet, at the outpipe from the winery destalker, may smell of almond.) Blackcurrant sometimes continues its more floral notes, more rarely attenuating to redcurrant character. I am reminded of a recent lunch in Paris, which concluded with a dish of redcurrants. The very next day, the moment the cork came out of a 1947 Brane Cantenac, there was the fragrance of redcurrants again. No wonder Serena Sutcliff speaks of 'a noseful of Cabernet Sauvignon'.

Complexity

Why are the flavour and bouquet of Cabernet Sauvignon so complex? Differences between Cabernet and other varieties are quite readily observed by inspecting the vine and tasting the wine, but at the chemical level it is quite impossible to distinguish between different varieties because of the close genetic relationship between different cultivars of *Vitis vinifera* (67). All red wines of this species contain virtually the same anthocyanins, phenolics, sugars, organic acids, amino acids, minerals, and other elements. The differences are quantitative rather than qualitative, and rather reminiscent of the little girl who said she liked boy chocolate dolls best because they have that little bit more chocolate!

Among the most important reasons for the supremacy of Cabernet is that its acid, alcohol, and tannic qualities permit it to have a long life. The major role of aging is to increase the complexity of a wine. Singleton (66) gives the example of ethyl alcohol, and three other different higher primary alcohols in a wine being oxidised in the course of aging. These would oxidise to four aldehydes, and then they in turn would field four carboxy acids. Each of the acids would esterify with a remaining portion of each of the initial alcohols, and create a total of sixteen different esters. With the remaining alcohols and acids, a total of twenty-eight substances would have developed from the original four. There are over four hundred grape constituents (37), and so, when the above mathematics and chemistry are applied to this number, the potential flavour components are incalculable: complexity complexed. Ponder that, O ye synthesisers and sophisticators!

Cabernet Sauvignon wines are frequently matured in new oak casks, and this introduces confusion in the recognition of the intrinsic odour of Cabernet

Sauvignon. Some forests produce an oak which, when coopered, has a minty character in the spearmint to peppermint range. It can be difficult to distinguish the mint character of, for example, Nevers oak, from Cabernet Sauvignon (45). In Mouton-Rothschilds before 1953, there was an odour note suggesting camphor. In the 1953 wines, for the first time, this was replaced by mint. Was this a change in oak?

Hermitage/black Shiraz, matured in this new oak, can sometimes perplex the taster, especially on the nose. This confluence between Cabernet and new wood character in wines is difficult to many at masked tastings. An explanation may be forthcoming (41). Peak number 48, in the gas liquid chromatographic flow, is due to 4-Hydroxy-3-Methyloctanoic acid gamma-lactone (IIA or IIB) (Furanone). Webb considered this 'whiskey lactone' (as the Japanese call it) was most likely extracted from the oak barrel during aging. So there you are. It could still be an intrinsic part of the Cabernet flavour profile. What is certain is that it is a strong component of its bottle character.

Other claimants for the characteristic aroma of Cabernet Sauvignon are n-octanol and 2-methoxy-3-isobutyl pyrazine (6) but even they probably are not an isolated duet. At present we disciples can but follow Somers' view, that the consistency of varietal character probably is due to the production of several constituents in favourable amounts and proportions under the control of dominant genes, unless overshadowed by the effects of climate and micro-climate on vine physiology.

Comparison of Cabernet Sauvignon and Merlot (unfortunately partly from the poor 1963 vintage in France (15), showed important differences between the quantities of several components of the gas chromatographic flow. Cabernet Sauvignon and Merlot wines with some of the same odour characteristics differ three or even five to one in component analysis.

Some of the differences are notable. Gamma-butyrolactone is only half as strong in Cabernet as in Merlot. Ethyl caprate is considerably less in Cabernet, but isoamyl lactate is nearly six times stronger, while diethyl succinate was in four times greater concentration.

Somers' gel columns show similar differences in a comparison of Cabernet Sauvignon and Malbec with other varieties. Levels of tannin pigment and total anthocyanins were twice as high as other varieties tested. The pigment profiles of young varietal wines (Appendix X) (68) gave an exceptionally high level of tannin pigments for both Cabernet Sauvignon and Malbec, and a very high level of total anthocyanins for Cabernet Sauvignon. On another occasion the colour intensity and ionisation of anthocyanins of Cabernet Sauvignon bore a direct relation to quality assessment. It is nice to know that our palates are on the right track.

Another dimension of complexity, discussed elsewhere, is the fact that the size of Cabernet Sauvignon wines varies, and this can also apply within a district or even a vineyard.

Finally, there is a difference among clones of what is quite definitely the same variety. In 1973, CSIRO experimental winemaker George Kerridge showed a run of small batch fermented Sauvignon wines, from some famous Australian clones like 125 and 126, with, among others, a recent Bordeaux import. This was said to have marked infection with leaf roll virus. On tasting the wines masked, it was to be expected that the high-producing Australian selection made a wine with the typical clarity and 'cut' of Cabernet Sauvignon. What did surprise, however, was that the French clone made a wine of more supple middle flavour.

Some of the reasons for the extraordinary flavour spectrum of Cabernet Sauvignon wines may now be more apparent. I believe there is no more complex wine made from a single variety. This complexity, with an infinite variety of attractive, even exciting odours and flavours, is the secret of Cabernet Sauvignon's charm for the connoisseur.

Size

In *Alice Through the Looking Glass*, Humpty Dumpty said 'When *I* use a word, it means just what I choose it to mean, neither more nor less.' Thus it is with size, which seems to mean so many different things in relationship to wine.

Wines, like people, are infinitely variable biological systems. They can be young or old, sweet or dry, sound or sour, big or little. And so may the taster vary, with the result that there are very few absolutes. The question of size for instance. A person or a wine can be long or short, thick or thin, generous or stingy, radiant or austere, bucolic or sophisticated. Both dimension and 'personality' are describable.

Jacquelin and Poulain (34) sized the clarets of the five principal communes of the Médoc. Michael Broadbent (17) has worked out a chart intended 'to throw the relative dryness, sweetness and weight or body of wine into visual perspective'. Evans and Halliday (28) have done something similar with Australian wines.

In sizing Australian Cabernets for the 1976 J. K. Walker lecture by flavour profile analysis methods (19), wines of every Australian region were graded. There are a number of reasons why that portion of the lecture is not included at this time. Size is only a part of quality. How much is due to the variety of Cabernet, clonal differences, other grapes, production per acre, stage of ripeness, etc? Soil and micro-climate, even within a vineyard, can and will cause wide variation. Furthermore, this small book on Cabernet is not the place to integrate space-time, computers, and the neurology of taste; friends like John Beeston,

Peter Joyce and Jack Shipton and others who have assisted my labours will, hopefully, see the result in *The Style of the Taster*.

Suffice it here to record there are two poles of Cabernet flavour volume. On the one hand, the wine may be moderately light to delicate, with a certain meagre hollowing out of the middle, leading up to a rather firm and tannic finish. Some might be amused to call it the doughnut style, with the hole in the middle. On the other hand, the wine may be quite generous and rich right through, with perhaps an intensification of flavour volume before a less obviously firm finish. These two styles depend more on regional and climatic differences than on winemaking. For example, almost all of the wines made in a cold year in Bordeaux are of the former style, unless they have been subject to some very sophisticated handling. From the regional point of view, one might think of the first style as being typical of the Cabernets of Cantenac, Bordeaux; Hawkes Bay, New Zealand; or Seaview, South Australia. The second style is illustrated by the Cabernets of St Julien, Bordeaux; many wines of the Napa Valley in California, or those of Clare in South Australia. Extremes of size are discussed further in winemaking.

> *Athenaeus tells on one occasion, someone put a very little wine into a wine cooler and said it was sixteen years old. Gnathaena replied, 'It is very small for its age.'*
> —Diepnosophists

Finish

Here, finish loosely refers to the last taste of the wine in the mouth (end palate for the purists) plus the cut-off of flavour by the astringency of the 'tannin'. This latter can be mouth-puckering in youthful wines. In better wines the former reappears in altered form when the mouth is empty, and none has a more prolonged *aftertaste* than good Cabernet Sauvignon. Whether to regard this afterglow as part of the finish is up to you.

In any red wine, the puckering astringency may be increased by skin, pip, and stalk contact and damage during winemaking; these are the sources of pigments and tannic compounds which impart bitterness and astringency to the finish of a red. The winemaker is in a good position to control these aspects of flavour, by regulation of skin contact times, and the use of fermented grape skin pressings, presswine as opposed to free run. Later, new oak tannin will add a further dimension of bitterness and astringency, to be cautiously metered in Cabernet wine because a fine and balanced finish is an intrinsic and natural part of the free run wine. Very little Art is needed for top Cabernet grapes.

> *The whole Science of Art is Selection*
> Lady Mary Stewart

CHAPTER FOUR

Winemaking

Trout once wrote a short story which was a dialogue between two pieces of yeast. They were discussing the possible purposes of life as they ate sugar and suffocated in their own excrement. Because of their limited intelligence, they never came close to guessing that they were making champagne.

—Kurt Vonnegut Jnr, *Breakfast of Champions.*

The making of Cabernet wines will be covered by comment on varieties, fermentation and maturation.

There have been fashions in the *encépagement* (the mixing of varieties) of vintages involving Cabernet Sauvignon; from the twenty-seven varieties of last century, to current practice in Bordeaux; Cabernet there now forms almost all of the wine to less than half. If there were no Cabernet, there would be no great Bordeaux. (See Appendix II, Table 3A.)

In Australia as in California, the variety has been made and bottled, straight without addition, although more frequently blended. A friend of Peter Joyce was informed 'there's no straight Cabernet, it's always mixed with Sauvignon'. Among the Bordeaux of early last century, 'Lafitte was improved by the addition of worthy robust red Hermitage.' In 1787, Jefferson was able to write 'the wines of . . . Chateau Margau, La Tour de Ségur, and Houtbrion, are not in perfection till 4 years old; de la Fite, somewhat lighter . . . good at 3 years . . . all . . . begin to decline at about 7 years old.' (35.) Varieties and winemaking of the day are difficult to ascertain now. Some winemakers have used Cabernet as an essence to lend more complexity to our standard Australian Shiraz/Hermitage wines; others have added small amounts of one or more varieties to modify the palate of a Cabernet wine, or to make it quicker maturing, as in France.

Now that reliability of labelling is virtually established in Australia, we are seeing the emergence of consistent Cabernet styles in which the mixtures, or the use of 'straight' wine, depend on the skill of the winemaker and acceptance by the connoisseur. In both groups there are many more talented people than a quarter of a century ago.

Both Kelly and Guyot commented on the extraordinary bigness achieved by some Cabernets, in contrast to the 'doughnut' style. The local outcome of this, at times, in Australia, has been to fashion a vintage port. Two of these, the 1925 Seven Hill and the 1945 Stonyfell, have been magnificent examples. At the other pole, Cabernet material has been so light, in a certain area and season, that prudence indicated a rosé. Sandalford is the pick of the bunch but Houghton's, Coriole, McWilliams', Seppelt's and Mildara have marketed particularly attractive pink Cabernet wines. Like the great Beaulieu Cabernet rosé of California, or the Lascombe rosé from Bordeaux, they are for the serious winelover, and not sweet or pickly like a seducer's potion.

When the season provides absolutely perfect grapes they make their own wines, not the rule in my Australian experience. The technique of fermenting a Cabernet wine is very like designing a building or a painting. It takes a lot of knowledge and a fair amount of discipline. Education and experience provide the former, and sensitivity calibrates the latter. It recalls the story of the *touriste* buying a very *chic*, very simple, black gown in a Paris *salon*. Rather taken with it, she paled on hearing the price. 'Why so much?' she asked. 'Madame is paying for the restraint,' she was informed.

The possible variations, apart from degree of ripeness and the use of related varieties to enhance balance and increase complexity of flavour, relate to temperature of fermentation, the study and use of cultivated yeast and the flavour thereof, open or closed fermenting vessels, and so on.

On a visit to Chateau Latour at vintage in 1967, there were rows of closed stainless steel fermenters alongside the open oak *cuves*. When the winemaker noted my surprise at seeing tradition so discarded, he was kind enough to arrange a tasting run of wines since the steel had been introduced. He invited a comment on which had been fermented in the wood, and which in the steel. I couldn't tell the difference, and he replied 'Neither can we.' Bully for Latour.

Students of Australian winemaking should observe the differences in flavour of Cabernet fermented by the standard three methods in use here: plunged in open tanks; skins headed down under wooden rafts; or in closed steel fermenters.

The maker's influence on finish of the wine is discussed under flavour.

It is in the maturation of Cabernet Sauvignon wines that the greatest influence of the winemaker is brought to bear. Intrigued by the relationship of oak flavour to Cabernet Sauvignon, I tried a small quantity of wine for six months in a steel vessel, without any wood contact at all. There was no question that the wine had developed certain characters we tend to associate with the use of new oak maturation; its own 'cedar' or 'cigar box' type of development with just a hint of the 'whisky lactone' character previously mentioned. But what a pale shadow of the same wine matured in new oak! The wood gives a strong shading to the natural flavour profile of the grape, accentuates various elements of bouquet and finish, and really fleshes the skeleton.

The other critical function of wood maturation is to permit a slow and controlled oxidation, which is exactly what Cabernet Sauvignon needs to develop its marvellous definitive characters. On one occasion, an open can of blackcurrant syrup was forgotten at the back of the refrigerator. After some months it had developed some of the cedar bouquet which one associates with mature Cabernet wine. Perhaps this is a good example of the effects of slow oxidation on aroma of a fruit related to the Sauvignon grape. This can take place in larger and/or older wooden vessels to produce one type of Cabernet wine, preferred by many. A different style, typically seen in the great Bordeaux, is obtained from time in new and smaller oaken casks, with a vigorous pickup of oak derivatives. The winemaker of experience learns to let the Sauvignon make its own statement each season, sometimes assisting it to become more audible.

Provenance: reliability of label

Expert: from 'x', the unknown; Spurt: a drip under pressure

The separation of Australian red table wines into *claret* and *burgundy* became common after the first World War. The trend has only now been halted. The 1965 Adelaide Wine Show specifications stated: 'AUSTRALIAN CLARET: A dry red table wine which may vary from fairly dark to light red in colour according to the age of the wine and from light to medium body. The acidity and body should be well balanced and the wine, whilst soft and rounded on the middle palate should finish firm and astringent and showing, as well as grape tannin flavour, some but not excessive flavour of oak tannin from the maturation wood. The bouquet should be fruity and in harmony with the body and flavour of the wine. An amber colour is objectionable. The alcoholic strength should be between 17 per cent and 25 per cent proof spirit.

AUSTRALIAN BURGUNDY: A dry red table wine of colour and body similar to Claret but a softer wine which may be of somewhat lower acidity and which must be soft and round on the middle palate and lack the characteristic astringency of Claret on the finish. The alcoholic strength should be between 17 per cent and 25 per cent proof spirit.'

Of historical interest is the 1967 (2) suggestion, never implemented, that 'California claret be a dry red table wine of about 11.5 per cent alcohol, and *at least* 0.65 per cent total acidity, and California burgundy a wine of 12.5 per cent alcohol, or more, and not over 0.65 per cent total acidity.' The Wine Institute subsequently specified 'California claret should be light to medium red in colour, tart, of light or medium body,' and 'California burgundy should be medium to deep red in colour and full bodied.'

A Cabernet Sauvignon varietal class is judged in exhibitions at Adelaide, McLaren Vale, Mudgee, Riverland, Rutherglen, Lilydale, Hobart and Barossa in Australia, and is well established in California and New Zealand. There is debate about the value of wine exhibitions in Australia, but the State Agricultural Societies support them and the public considers them, by and large, to be reliable indicators of quality wines.

During the last century, most Australian wines were labelled by variety, district, and usually the vineyard (13) (50). It is possible that this changed when vineyards all over the country started to concentrate on a number of specific types of 'known' wines, instead of sticking to what each vineyard did best and in the most natural way. The nadir was reached with the same wine labelled either as claret or burgundy. One large firm actually did this (43).

Connoisseurs led the revolt. Just as Pinot Noir in Burgundy could make a full soft round wine like Musigny, or an austere firmer finishing one like Corton, so Cabernet could make a rich, fruity, St Emilion or an austere firm Cantenac. It was obvious that one either would have to learn what Cabernet did where, or rely on someone with that knowledge. Varietal labelling is good semantics and there can be a lifetime's pleasure in the instruction.

In the past, without regulation, some wines labelled Cabernet Sauvignon quite obviously had little or no character of the grape. Whether this was simple dishonesty, or the use of grapes from overcropped vines, was not always so obvious. The latter course remains open. Regulatory control in Australia still refers only to truth in district and varietal labelling. To carry a label, the wine must contain at least eighty per cent grapes of the appropriate district or variety. This seems reasonable and is far preferable to the situation in California, where, as far as variety is concerned, fifty-one per cent is sufficient to permit legal labelling. More surprisingly, the wine needs only to be *made* in the relevant region. The grapes do not necessarily have to be *grown* there. That is definitely illegal in Australia. Any wine that you now see, fairly recently made, and labelled with the variety Cabernet Sauvignon and the district, should be O.K.

The French, with a thousand years' head start, have arranged matters even better. Not only have they limited the varieties which can be used to make an area's wine, but there is a moderately well-policed control of per acre production. The penalty is that overproduction, by definition, cannot be sold at the best price. And few wines reflect production levels more than Cabernet. I have yet to see definitive varietal character over six tons per acre, and it is generally only good, not great, at half this level. The great Sauvignon flavours come in the range of one to three tons per acre, give or take a fraction.

The situation in France is confused at the moment, apart from the 1973 *scandale du vin*. Advances in technology, and clonal selection, have raised production to a marked degree, and the growers now exert pressure for upward revision by the State of the per acre production allowed.

The consumer should keep in mind, in our relentless pursuit of honesty and reliability, that straight regional Cabernet Sauvignon wine may in fact not be as attractive on the palate as one which has been ameliorated by other varieties, as in Bordeaux. Outstanding cellar styles here in Cabernet are developing, just as they did with Shiraz/Hermitage and multiple district blending.

New to wine, I earnestly pursued single district, single variety wines, wishing to learn regional flavours, and not realising that master blenders were sometimes able to make better, often magnificent wines, by balancing wines of widely different varieties and vineyards. Even then, Maurice O'Shea warned with the news that one would be lucky to find a single district wine, however labelled! Some of Australia's best selling wines nowadays are cellar styles which have been developed over the years. The blending may be of districts, or varieties, or of vineyards within a district; or, as in Bordeaux, within the same or nearby vineyards, within the eighty per cent restriction imposed.

It is striking to see a parallel emergence in modern Bordeaux individual reds of a 'house style': certain flavour elements common to wines of different Chateaux, under the same ownership. This was as well known in Burgundy as in Australia, where many serious tasters can pick the company or house which has bottled the masked red wine before them, wherever the contents may have originated. No loss of quality is implied, whatever are the conclusions as to cause, but one is surprised to see it appearing in that fount of individuality, Bordeaux.

A current school of thought is expressed by Doug Seabrook (62), one of the great palates of Australia. 'I am always puzzled by an industry that bluffs itself into thinking that the consumer will continue to accept the passing off of only eighty per cent! [Cabernet]. There is a mediocrity about it which no purist can accept, especially as it is demonstrably unnecessary.'

With increased experience as a student and winemaker, I have come to a different opinion: that another decade will see the firm establishment in Australia of regional Cabernet styles. That is, wines of indeed straight Cabernet; *or* blends where Cabernet is the major variety by volume; *or* cellar styles where some Cabernet is added to give complexity to one or more other varieties which form the major proportion of the wine. The connoisseur should be reassured that this is now in the pursuit of excellence, and not to deceive for profit.

Classification

Australian vineyards and technology currently are in a state of flux, and a definitive assessment of our Cabernet wines lies in the future.

Before the current regulations in Australia, one of the difficulties was to find out exactly where the Cabernet in particular wines came from. For example, much of the material in the extraordinary clarets from Yalumba, and Seppelt's Great Western bottled Cabernets of the early 1950s, appeared to have come, in part at least, from the Barossa Valley. The Hardy clarets of the same era obtained their Cabernet from McLaren Vale or Coonawarra. Any Cabernet in the early Penfold range of St Henri and Grange, could have come from Kalimna. Where did the Cabernet come from in the velvet 1965 Basedow claret and where does that material go now? Or the Cabernet in those superb Reynella clarets of the late 1930s and 1940s? Or the 1950s of Mildara Cabernet Shiraz? Even in an area of which I have close knowledge, it can be difficult to trace the origin of some of the best Cabernets. Much of it is grown on properties which do not have a winery.

Consider the situation in France. With typically Gallic compromise, the classifications of 1647, 1767, and 1855 and even the revised 1973, are basically on what a bottle of wine fetches on the open market. Even so, one could never understand why vineyards like Meyney, Gloria, Lanessan, etc. missed out in the great growths. What were the Rauzans doing up there when Cantemerle and Talbot were languishing? How did the Countess and the Baron continue to lie side by side? How could each member of the Léoville trinity be equally holy? In the days of decline of Haut Brion, why did no one speak up for Domaine du Chevalier? And so on. There were a lot of cunning palates, who were prepared to bid up for Cheval Blanc, even though it got its guernsey only fairly recently. But the French are great realists, and there is a new Bordeaux classification afoot in which there will be only three groups. The first group will contain the nine Greats: Lafite, Mouton, Latour, Haut Brion, Margaux, Cheval Blanc, Pétrus, Ausone, and Yquem. Every other classified growth would be in the second group, with a third for the rest.

There have been attempts, of a sort, at an Australian classification. In an appendix to André Simon's book on Australian wine (64), Victor Gibson made a list of the commercially available wines that he considered the highest quality, together with their prices. There were twenty-three on the list and twelve firms represented. Nine had Cabernet as a varietal component on the label and at least four others were known to contain Cabernet.

Some years before this (42) I essayed a broad classification of Australian Cabernets. When it was later revised, among the *Classic Wines of Australia*, it met with a modicum of acceptance. No ranking was undertaken, and the classification was merely implied. Cabernet grapes from the Adelaide, Barossa, Clare, Coonawarra, Southern Vales, North and Central Victoria, and Swan Valley initiated 'clarets', or varietally named popular blends, in the fifties. From that opus of the days of innocence (43), here are the wine firms: All Saints, Amery Browns Milawa, Burings, Glenloth, Hamiltons, Hardys, Houghtons, Metala, Mildara, Orlando, Penfolds, Quelltaler, Reynella, Rhine Castle, Rouge Homme, Ryecroft, Saltram, Sandalford, Seabrooks, Seaview, Seppelts, Seven Hills, Stanley, Stonyfell, Tahbilk, Woodleys, Wynns, and Yalumba.

Honoured to launch Dan Murphy's excellent *Classification of Australian Wines* (51), in November 1974, I remarked how brave he was to stick his neck out so invitingly. Australian winelovers are in his debt for attempting so formidable a task, and achieving so much. It will certainly serve as a base for future consideration. The vineyards he listed market over 100 wines containing Cabernet. Len Evans (27) has a similar if less dogmatic collection. What a nice research program it would be even to list the acreage in production of these, when they are stable.

Current prices (Appendix I) give some indication of the number of Australian wines with Cabernet, and their market valuation. Auction prices in general tend to confirm. It would be rather ironic, but not surprising, if the future classification falls most naturally into place on price.

CHAPTER FIVE

Coda

Le raisin sans défaut
—de Secondat

And so ends this humble tribute to a miracle of nature: Cabernet, the exquisite paradox. Sauvignon. The very name harks of redemption, except that it derives from *sauvage*. Paradox indeed!

There is cause for reflection in that the beautiful Cabernet wines have had their genesis in one shoot of one vine, without sexual means, for a thousand or more years. From Gaul to the New World, even unto Terra Australis. The hard vine, the iron vine. A difficult infant, a ravishing *Gran'dame*, forgiving all offence if you but attend to what it tells. One hundred and fifty days and nights to fashion complexity as limitless as the stars.

Such wine might well be called perfect. 'Like the perfect wife, it looks nice and it is nice. Natural; wholesome; even helpful, yet not assertive, dependable always; gracious and gentle but neither dull, dumb, nor monotonous: a rare gift and a real joy.' (65.) And may it be added, like a loving woman, however difficult it may be at times, once you learn its moods it gives, and gives, and gives.

There is still some distance to travel towards the great future that mankind will one day create. May this offering on Cabernet be a small voice to help in your enjoyment of the voyage.

In keeping with the paradoxical nature of the subject of this book the author mentions that surgeons, following McBurney, remove appendices. Here one, led by Dionysus, inserts a few.

Appendices

APPENDIX I

Australian Vineyard Cabernets

Precision and a complete list are impossible due to inflation, discounting and other factors, quite beyond the author's capacity. Prices are average $Australian retail, per 750 ml bottle, Cabernet Sauvignon unless otherwise stated, May 1977.

Anakie, Geelong	$3.50
Angle Vale Ltd 1974, Angle Vale	2.94
Angoves, Murray River	2.82
Arrowfield, Upper Hunter	2.80
Augustine, Mudgee	—
Balgownie, Bendigo, 1974	4.20
J. B. & T. N. Barry, Clare. Cabernet Shiraz 1973	4.20
Basedow, Barossa, Cabernet Shiraz	—
Belbourie, Lower Hunter	—
Bellevue, Lower Hunter Cabernet Hermitage	2.45
Berri Co-operative, Murray River, 1974	2.31
Wolf Blass, Cabernet Shiraz 1974, cellar style	6.77
Bleasdale, Langhorne Creek 1972	4.12
Botolobar, Mudgee	2.90
D. Bowden, Coonawarra. Cabernet Shiraz 1975	3.50
Brands Laira, Coonawarra 1975	3.95

Brokenwood, Lower Hunter. Cabernet Shiraz	4.70
Brown Bros., Milawa. Shiraz Cabernet	3.38
Buller, Rutherglen	2.33
Buller's Beverford, Swan Hill	2.10
Campbell's, Rutherglen, Cabernet Shiraz	—
Chambers, Rutherglen	3.00
Chateau Douglas, Upper Hunter. Cabernet Shiraz	2.59
Chateau Lorraine d'Entre Casteaux Tasmanian bottled	—
Chateau Yarringa, Lilydale	—
Chateau Tahbilk, Tabilk, 1973	2.89
1970	8.00
Clarevale, Clare	3.30
Paul Conte, Wanneroo	3.20
Mt Barker	3.00
Coriole, Southern Vales. Cabernet Shiraz	3.25
Craigmoor, Mudgee	3.36
Crittenden, Kalimna 1963–70	10.00
D'Arenberg, Southern Vales 1972	4.01
De Bortoli, Murrumbidgee River	2.04
Elliotts, Lower Hunter	2.75
Hamiltons, McLaren Vale 1973	4.04

39

Nildottie 1973	3.07
Nildottie Cabernet Shiraz 1973	3.60
Springton 1973	3.54
Heemskerk, Tamar Valley 1976	—
Henke, Yarck 1974	5.00
Henschke, Cabernet Shiraz	—
Hermitage, Lower Hunter	—
Hillside, Lower Hunter 1975	2.50
Hoffmans, Barossa. Cabernet Shiraz	3.75
Hollydene, Upper Hunter 1974	3.53
Horderns, Upper Hunter, Cabernet Mataro 1975	2.63
Houghtons, Swan	2.71
Hungerford Hill, Lower Hunter	2.67
Huntingdon Estate, Mudgee	4.00
James Cook, South Australian Co-operative	2.75
Kaiser Stuhl, Barossa Co-operative Cabernet Shiraz 1973	3.25 3.74
Karlsburg	4.06
Karrawirra, Barossa Cabernet Shiraz 1973	3.06 3.74
Kay Bro., Southern Vales. Amery Cabernet Shiraz 1972	2.67
Krondorf, Barossa. Shiraz Cabernet	2.42
Lake's Folly, Lower Hunter 1976 Light Dry Red 1976	4.50 3.25
La Provence Cabernet Pinot Tasmanian bottled	—
Leo Buring, cellar style 1972 Karadoc 3 litre	3.12 5.82
Lindemans, Coonawarra 1966 Shiraz Cabernet 1972 Watervale Shiraz Cabernet 1966 Coonawarra 1973	6.94 3.94 8.03 3.98
McManus, Murrumbidgee River 1973	2.21
McPhersons, Lower Hunter Shiraz Cabernet 1974	2.00
McWilliams, Mount Pleasant 1968 Murrumbidgee River	4.65 2.80
Marienberg, Southern Vales, Shiraz Cabernet 1973	3.00
Merrivale	3.00
Middleton's Mt. Mary, Lilydale	—
Mildara, cellar style Cabernet Shiraz Coonawarra 1972 Coonawarra Cabernet Shiraz Malbec 1973	2.87 4.30 3.25

Montrose, Mudgee	2.79
Morris, Rutherglen	4.20
Mudgee Wines, Mudgee	4.20
A. Norman, Angle Vale, Cabernet Shiraz	3.54
Orlando, Barossa	3.48
Jacobs Creek, cellar style	2.10
Osicka, Central Victoria	3.75
W. & S. Pannell, Margaret River	3.00
Penfolds, cellar styles of Cabernet Shiraz	4.75
St Henri (may include Mataro)	7.21
Pirramimma, Southern Vales, Cabernet Shiraz	3.10
Queldinburg, Upper Hunter	3.05
Redman, Coonawarra 1975 magnum	10.96
Renmano, Murray River Cabernet Malbec	2.26 1.96
Reynella, Southern Vales Pokolbin, Shiraz Cabernet	5.35 2.08
Richard Hamilton, Southern Vales 1974	3.67
Rosemount, Upper Hunter 1975	2.98
Rosetto, Murrumbidgee River 1973	1.79
Rothbury Estate, Lower Hunter 1975	2.75
Ryecroft, Southern Vales 1973	3.07
Saltram, Mamre Brook Shiraz Cabernet cellar style	5.48 2.42
Saltrams 1976	4.00
San Bernadino, Murrumbidgee River. Cabernet Shiraz	2.00
Sandalford, Swan. Cabernet Shiraz 1974	2.84
Saxonvale, Lower Hunter 1975	2.85
Seaview, Southern Vales Cabernet Shiraz	4.34 3.65
Seppelts, Dorrien 1972 Great Western 1972 Hermitage Cabernet, cellar style	3.90 — 2.84
Sevenhill, Clare. Cabernet Shiraz 1972	3.85
Southern Vales Wines, Southern Vales Co-operative Shiraz Cabernet	2.90 2.64
Stanley, Clare Cabernet Malbec Cabernet Shiraz Watervale Shiraz Cabernet	6.10 3.80 3.25 2.70

Stanton & Killeen, Rutherglen,
Cabernet Shiraz —

Stonyfell, Langhorne Creek. Metala
  Cabernet Shiraz 4.23
  Hermitage Cabernet cellar style 2.42

Sutherland Smith, Rutherglen. 10%
  Cabernet 90% Shiraz 2.73
  30% Cabernet, 70% Shiraz 3.27

Taranga, Southern Vales 2.89

Taylors, Clare 1974 2.87

Thomas Hardy, cellar style 5.81
  Southern Vales 7.21
  Cellar style Shiraz Cabernet 2.51

Tim Knapstein's Enterprise, Clare,
Cabernet Shiraz $3.10

Tolleys, Barossa 2.77
  Cabernet Shiraz 2.41

Torresan, Southern Vales. Shiraz
  Cabernet 1972 2.88

Tullochs, Lower Hunter 1973 4.50

Tyrrells, Lower Hunter Cabernet

Shiraz 1974 2.37

Vasse Felix, Margaret River 3.00

Waldeck, Swan 2.68
  Cabernet Hermitage 2.12

Wantirna Estate,
  Melbourne/Dandenong 4.00

Wendouree, Clare. Cabernet Shiraz
  Malbec 3.65

Wollundry, Lower Hunter,
  Hermitage Cabernet —

Wyndham Estate, Lower Hunter
  1975 2.85
  Cabernet Shiraz 1974 2.45

Wynns, Coonawarra 4.89
  Cabernet Hermitage 3.59

Yaldara, Barossa. Cabernet Shiraz
  1970 2.79

Yalumba, cellar styles (named
  bottlings) 3.52

Yarra Yering, Lilydale 4.00

Yeringberg, Lilydale 2.50

APPENDIX II

FRANCE

The following lists are from a monumental tasting organised by Gault-Millau (*). Thirty-six professionals tasted some 48 Bordeaux, with instructive results. They especially emphasise the fallacy of 'good' and 'bad' years in vintage charts—'a dreadful trap.' Certain vineyards are remarkably consistent, others not. (Many are named in both groups.) And finally, as there was an averaged assessment of only 4 vintages (1966, 1970, 1971, 1973) of each wine, with some likely contenders not represented, Gault-Millau are ready to begin again.

TABLE 1A

8 'Super-grands'. Caves Nicolas, 1970 vintage.
Index converted to 100 for first place.

Ch. Latour	100
Ch. Mouton-Rothschild	96.2
Ch. Lafite-Rothschild	94.2
Ch. Petrus	93.6
Ch. Cheval-Blanc	92.4
Ch. Haut-Brion	91.2
Ch. Ausone	88.8
Ch. Margaux	84.3

*Ref. Le Nouveau Guide Gault-Millau
    Jan. 1977 p.26 Vins de Bordeaux: le test du siècle

TABLE 2A

Tasting Panel ranking of 48 Bordeaux vintages 1966, 1970, 1971, 1973. (Prices listed in Le Nouveau Guide, Gault-Millau)

Ch. Calon-Ségur	3e Grand Cru Classe (Médoc) St Estephe	17.7
Ch. Gloria	Bourgeois (Médoc) St Julien	16.9
Ch. Grand-Barrail-Lamarzelle-Figeac	Grand Cru Classe (St Emilion)	16.5
Ch. Bel-Air-Marquis d'Aligre	Bourgeois Supérieur Exceptionnel (Médoc) Soussans (Ht Médoc)	15.9
Ch. Clos des Jacobins	Grand Cru Classe (St Emilion)	15.2
Ch. Haut-Bailly	Grand Cru Classe (Graves Léognan	14.9
Ch. Durfort-Vivens	2e Grand Cru Classe (Médoc Margaux)	14.5
Ch. Fourcas-Hosten	Bourgeois Supérieur (Médoc) Listac (Ht Médoc)	14.4
Ch. Haut-Batailley	5e Grand Cru (Médoc) Pauillac	14.2
Ch. Gruaud-Larose	2e Grand Cru Classe (Médoc) St Julien	14.2
Ch. Dassault	Grand Cru Classe (St Emilion)	14.1
Ch. Clos René	Pomerol	14.1
Ch. Lascombes	2e Grand Cru Classe (Médoc Margaux)	14
Ch. Tailhas	Pomerol	14
Ch. Canon	1er Grand Cru Classe 'b' (St Emilion)	14
Ch. Duhart-Milon-Rothschild	4e Grand Cru Classe (Médoc) Pauillac	13.8
Ch. Talbot	4e Grand Cru Classe (Médoc) St Julien	13.7
Ch. L'Angélus	Grand Cru Classe (St Emilion)	13.6
Ch. La Gaffelière	1er Grand Cru Classe 'b' (St Emilion)	13.6
Ch. de Ferrand	St Emilion Grand Cru	13.6
Ch. Mouton-Baron-Philippe	5e Grand Cru Classe (Médoc) Pauillac	13.5
Ch. Larcis-Ducasse	Grand Cru Classe (St Emilion)	13.5
Ch. Poujeaux (Theil)	Bourgeois Supérieur (Médoc) Moulis (Ht Médoc)	13.2
Ch. Lynch-Bages	5e Grand Cru Classe (Médoc)	13.1
Ch. Grace-Dieu (Pauty)	St Emilion	13.1
Ch. Balestard-La-Tonnelle	Grand Cru Classe (St Emilion)	13
Ch. Lanessan	Bourgeois Supérieur (Médoc) Cussac (Ht Médoc)	13
Ch. Nenin	Pomerol	13
Ch. Brane-Cantenac	2e Grand Cru Classe (Médoc) Cantenac (Màrgaux)	12.9
Ch. Bouscaut	Grand Cru Classe (Graves) Cadaujac	12.8
Ch. Grand-Puy-Lacoste	5e Grand Cru Classe (Médoc) Pauillac	12.7
Ch. Lagrange	3e Grand Cru Classe (Médoc) St Julien	12.5
Ch. de Sales	Pomerol	12.5
Ch. La Pointe	Pomerol	12.2
Ch. des Ormes-de-Pez	Bourgeois (Médoc) St Estephe (Ht Médoc)	12
Ch. Monbous-quet	St Emilion Grand Cru	12
Ch. Grand-Corbin-Despagne	Grand Cru Classe (St Emilion)	12

Ch. Cantenac	St Emilion Grand Cru	12
Ch. Malartic-la-Gravière	Grand Cru Classe (Graves) Léognan	12
Ch. La-Tour-de-By	Bourgeois (Médoc) Begadan (Bas-Médoc)	11.9
Ch. Phelan-Ségur	Bourgeois Supérieur (Médoc) St Estephe (Ht Médoc)	11.7
Ch. La Louvière	Graves (Léognan)	11.6
Ch. Larrivet-Haut-Brion	Graves (Léognan)	11.1
Ch. de Lescours	St Emilion	10.8
Ch. Bel-Orme-Tronquoy-de-Lalande	Bourgeois (Médoc) St Seurin-de-Cadourne (Ht Médoc)	10.7
Ch. Smith-Haut-Lafite	Grand Cru Classe (Graves) Martillac	10.6
Ch. La Mission-Haut-Brion	Grand Cru Classe (Graves) Talence	9.9
Ch. Chasse-Spleen	Bourgeois Supérieur Exceptionnel (Médoc) Moulis (Ht Médoc)	9.8

TABLE 3A

ENCEPAGEMENT (VARIETAL MIX, BORDEAUX)

Vineyard	Cabernet Sauvignon	Cabernet franc	Merlot	Petit-Verdot
Lafite	53–60	5–24	20–21	2–15
Latour	80	10	10	0
Mouton-Rothschild	88–90	5–7	3–4	1–3
Margaux	50–75	0–10	25–35	0–5
Haut-Brion	35–55	22–35	23–30	0
Petrus	0	10	90	0
Cheval Blanc	0	?67	33	?some
Ausone	34	33	33	0

% Acreage; after Gagnon (30), Penning-Rowsell (54), Ray (59, 60), etc.

N.B. Because per acre production varies with each variety and probably vineyard, these figures do not refer to varietal composition of the wines of the Chateaux.

If you don't have the experience, you must see the figures
Kerridge

APPENDIX III

CALIFORNIA

1973 Amateur Tasting (49)

	A	E
Inglenook 1966	1	6
Heitz 1966	2	3
Fetzer 1968	3	5
Spring Mountain 1968–9 *marriage*	4	4
Beaulieu Vineyards 1968	5	7
Robert Mondavi 1968	6	8
Christian Bros. N.V.	7	17
Ridge Vineyards 1967	8	1
Martin Ray 1966	9	2
Windsor Vineyards N.V.	10	13
Parducci 1968	11	9
Souverain 1967	12	14
Woodside-La Questa 1966	13	11
Novitiate N.V.	14	16
Buena Vista N.V.	15	15
Paul Masson N.V.	16	19
Almadén N.V.	17	20
Charles Krug 1967	18	11
Sebastiani N.V.	19	21
Louis Martini 1967	20	10
Mirassou 1968	21	18

A. Overall average ratings by several panels, including ladies. E. Sullivan's rating.

Fit to compete in this company are the Cabernets of Hallcrest (grapes now go elsewhere), Concannon, Weibel, Bertero and Pedroncelli. The more recently established Caymus and Sterling vineyards have made a great impact, but nothing like the following.

1976 Professional Tasting (36)

Six top Californian Cabernets (*) were recently masked and tasted by a professional-standard group against some classified French Growths, with the following result.

1. *Stag's Leap Wine Cellars '73
2. Chateau Mouton-Rothschild '70
3. Chateau Haut-Brion '70
4. Chateau Montrose '70
5. *Ridge 'Mountain Range' '71
6. Chateau Leoville-Las-Cases '71
7. *Mayacamas '71
8. *Clos du Val '72
9. *Heitz Cellar 'Martha's Vineyard' '70
10. *Freemark Abbey '69

* Bob Thompson, San Francisco, April 1977.

45

Appendix III contd.

Current Prices

Beaulieu Napa Valley, Georges de Latour 1972	$6.00	Sterling Vineyards Napa Valley 1972	4.75
Caymus Napa 1974	7.00	Chateau St. Jean Sonoma 1974	6.50
Chappellet Napa Valley 1973	7.50	Fetzer Mendocino 1974	6.00
Heitz Cellars Napa Valley, Martha's Vineyard 1972	15.00	Gundlach-Bundschu Sonoma 1974	4.50
		Parducci Mendocino 1971	4.25
Mayacamas Napa Valley 1972	8.00	Pedroncelli Sonoma 1973	3.50
Robert Mondavi Napa Valley 1973	6.00	Simi Alexander Valley 1972	4.95
Silver Oak North Coast 1972	6.00	Almaden California 1973	4.15
Spring Mountain Napa Valley 1974	7.50	Concannon Livermore Valley 1971	8.50
Stag's Leap Wine Cellars Napa Valley 1974	8.50	Mount Eden Santa Clara 1973, Lot 2	14.00
		Ridge Santa Clara 1973	8.50
		San Martin Santa Clara 1972	4.50

APPENDIX IV

NEW ZEALAND

Cabernet Sauvignon is the most widely planted red wine grape. 170 hectares in 1976. Frank Thorpy (74) lists the Cabernet wines made, 'but not necessarily available' from the makers.

Cooks
Corbans
Markovina
McWilliams
Mission
Montana
Nobilo's
Pacific
Penfolds
San Marino
Villa Maria
Western Vineyards

Current available (November 1976).

McWilliams Wines	$2.95 NZ
Seppelt-Vidals	$2.95 NZ
Villa Maria Wines	$2.95 NZ
Nobilo's Wines	$3.00 NZ
Montana Wines	$3.35 NZ
Cooks Wines	$4.00 NZ
	ex vineyard only

Cooks and McWilliams both have distinguished Show records. They are very well made, with excellent varietal character, firm acidity, inclining to the doughnut style. Oenological ambassador Thorpy has seen to it that I tasted the 1976 Gold Medal wines, and they show great potential development in bottle, of the 'cedar' cigar box so many admire.

APPENDIX V

Ripeness of Comparative Cabernets
(T.A. = Total Acidity as grams per litre tartaric)

C.S.I.R.O. Merbein (5) Region 4 irrigated

Date Harvest	8.3.74	4.3.75	25.2.76
Brix Sugar	22.9	22.8	22.4
pH	3.63	3.35	3.31
T.A.	4.6	5.2	5.6

Lake's Folly (Regions 4/5, but a rather special micro-climate non irrigated)

Date Harvest	2.3.74	13.3.75	24.2.76
Brix Sugar	20.5	20	20
pH	3.44	3.47	3.32
T.A.	6.75	6.93	7.09

McLaren Vale (Regions 3/4)*

Wine of	1974	1975	1976
Range of pH	3.70–4.30	3.50–4.08	3.58–4.07
	mean 4.09	mean 3.82	mean 3.81
T.A.	4.1–6.2	4.4–6.8	4.5–6.6
	mean 4.7	mean 5.2	mean 5.6

*Courtesy Dr Bryce Rankine, Australian Wine Research Institute.

Figures from 13–20 wines of the district.

APPENDIX VI

Production and winemaking figures of listed varieties
(Australian Bureau of Statistics)

Variety	\multicolumn{5}{c}{1975}					\multicolumn{5}{c}{1976}				
	NSW	Vic.	SA	WA	Aust.	NSW	Vic.	SA	WA	Aust.
BEARING AREA (Hectares)										
Cabernet Sauvignon	715	283	1377	79	2454	819	309	1607	89	2824
Grenache	416	286	5032	365	6099	395	269	4965	306	5935
Mataro (Morrastel)	143	57	1430	22	1652	157	64	1462	17	1700
Shiraz	3118	909	4350	234	8611	3220	919	4583	200	8922
TOTAL AREA (Hectares)										
Cabernet Sauvignon	944	493	2153	143	3733	992	553	2413	193	4151
Grenache	430	335	5328	390	6483	409	302	5264	326	6301
Mataro (Morrastel)	174	107	1628	22	1931	186	86	1635	17	1924
Shiraz	3399	1070	5297	294	10060	3468	1081	5576	262	10387
TOTAL PRODUCTION (Tonnes)										
Cabernet Sauvignon	4347	1803	9387	278	15815	4913	1897	10823	383	18016
Grenache	4894	2193	51073	1580	59740	4506	2171	37264	1413	45354
Mataro (Morrastel)	1532	367	12440	91	14430	1814	411	10683	64	12972
Shiraz	24968	7747	38426	934	72075	23828	7761	36880	908	69377

Variety	1975					1976				
	NSW	Vic.	SA	WA	Aust.	NSW	Vic.	SA	WA	Aust.
YIELD (Tonnes/Hectare)										
Cabernet Sauvignon	6080	6371	6817	3519	6445	5999	6139	6735	4303	6380
Grenache	11764	7668	10150	4329	9795	11408	8071	7505	4618	7642
Mataro (Morrastel)	10713	6439	8699	4136	8735	11554	6422	7307	3765	7631
Shiraz	8008	8523	8834	3991	8370	7400	8445		4540	
WINEMAKING (Tonnes)										
Cabernet Sauvignon	4347	1714	9387	278	15726	4913	1880	10823	383	17999
Grenache	4831	1979	50985	1571	59366	4436	2069	37218	1386	45109
Mataro (Morrastel)	1532	273	12404	76	14285	1730	382	10621		12733
Shiraz	24968	7437	38416	928	71749	22798	7559	36880	890	68127

Note: Queensland figures unavailable. Shiraz includes Black Shiraz, Red and Black Hermitage.

APPENDIX VII

CLIMATIC DATA

HEAT SUMMATION TABLE FOR CLASSIC WINE AREAS OF THE WORLD (33, 72)

Winkler
Region 1, Under 2500

Country	District	Degree Days (F)	(C)
Germany	Rheingau	1745	930
France	Auxerre	1850	1010
U.S.A.	Sonoma	2360	—
France	Beaune	2400	1380
France	Champagne	2449	—
Australia	Hobart	—	960
Australia	Launceston	—	1130

Region 2, 2501–3000

Country	District	(F)	(C)
France	Bordeaux	2519	—
New Zealand	Gisborne	—	1300
Portugal	Douro	2765	—
Australia	Barossa, S.A.	2838	—
U.S.A.	St Helena	2900	—

Region 3, 3001–3500

Country	District	(F)	(C)
Australia	Coonawarra, S.A.	3175	1270
Australia	Clare, S.A.	3231	1760
U.S.A.	Livermore	3260	—
Australia	Adelaide, S.A.	3458	—

Region 4, 3501–4000

Country	District	(F)	(C)
Australia	Gt Western, Stawell, Vic.	3505	—
Australia	Rutherglen, Vic.	3654	—
Australia	Berri, S.A.	3840	—
U.S.A.	Davis	3970	—

Region 5, Over 4000

Country	District	(F)	(C)
Australia	Swan Valley, W.A.	4079	—
Australia	Griffith, N.S.W.	4170	2230
Spain	Jerez de la Frontera	4194	—
Australia	Pokolbin, N.S.W.	4538	—
Algeria	Algiers	5200	—

APPENDIX VIII

AUSTRALIAN VINEYARD AREAS (26)

	Latitude	Altitude	Day-Degrees	Annual rainfall inches	Spring rainfall Sept.–Nov.	Ripening rainfall Feb.–Mar.	Av. humidity Oct.–April, relative %	Av. date last 36°F + 1 mean deviation
New South Wales								
Cessnock								
(Hunter River)	32°54′	40′	4228	27.7	6.0	5.1	—	Aug. 30
Griffith	34°17′	420′	4122	15.2	3.8	1.9	54	Sept. 22
Victoria								
Merbein	34°10′	185′	3945	9.7	2.3	1.4	55	Sept. 10
Rutherglen								
(Research Station)	36°06′	553′	3651	23.1	5.7	3.1	—	Sept. 27
Bendigo	36°46′	731′	3136	20.3	5.0	2.8	53	Sept. 13
Seymour	37°02′	464′	3044	22.2	5.6	3.0	61	Sept. 21
Stawell	37°03′	825′	2962	20.6	5.4	2.3	57	Aug. 1
Ararat	37°17′	1028′	2426	23.9	6.6	2.8	59	Aug. 6
Melbourne	37°49′	115′	2852	25.9	7.2	4.2	62	
Geelong	38°09′	90′	2659	21.3	6.1	3.3	69	July 16
South Australia								
Adelaide	34°56′	140′	3932	21.1	5.2	2.0	46	Nil
Berri	34°17′	215′	3856	9.8	2.5	1.2	49	July 29
Clare	33°50′	1300′	3192	24.1	6.1	2.0	53	Oct. 9
Nuriootpa								
(Barossa Valley)	—	—	2838	19.9	5.2	1.7	45	—
Coonawarra	—	—	2175	25.5	6.4	2.3	69	Oct. 20
Western Australia								
Guildford								
(Swan Valley)	31°53′	25′	4327	34.5	6.2	1.2	—	
Busselton	33°38′	9′	3235	34.0	6.3	1.5	—	Aug. 1
Manjimup	34°14′	917′	2587	42.6	9.8	2.2	65	Aug. 21
Mt Barker	34°36′	829′	2597	30.2	7.6	2.4	68	Aug. 19
Albany	35°02′	41′	2825	39.7	9.2	2.8	74	Nil

51

APPENDIX IX

SOME ANALYSES FROM THE LITERATURE

TABLE 1B (80)

Relative Concentrations of Acids (as Methyl Esters) in Extracts of Four Cabernet Wines

Peak No.	Acid[a]	Cabernet Sauvignon			Ruby Cabernet 1967
		1960, distilled		1955	
				CH_2Cl_2 ext.	CH_2Cl_2 ext.
		Aged	Unaged	Aged	Unaged
3	Me butyrate	+ + + +[b]	+ + +	+ + +	+ +
5	Me caproate	+ + + +	+ + + +	+ + + +	+ + +
6	Me lactate	+ +	?	+ +	+ + +
7	Me caprylate	+ + + +	+ + + +	+ + +	+ + +
12	Me 2-hydroxycaproate	—	—	+	+
15	Me 2-furoic	—	—	+ +	?
16	Dimethyl succinate	+ +	+ +	+ + + +	+ + + +
16A	Me caprate	+ + + +	+ + + +	+ + +	+ +
17A	Unk. hydroxy ester	?	—	—	+ +
18	Me 9-decenoate	+ + +	+ + +	—	—
19	Dimethyl glutarate	?	?	+	?
21	Me phenylacetate	?	—	+ +	?
22	Me salicylate	?	—	+ +	?

52

23	Unk. unsat. ester	?	?	+	+
26	Unk. hydroxy ester	—	—	+ + +	+ +
26A	Unk. hydroxy ester	—	—	+ +	—
33	Unk. unsat. ester	—	—	+ +	?
35	Dimethyl azelate	—	—	+	—
38	Me 3-phenyl-2-hydroxy-propionate	—	—	+ + +	?
48	Me vanillate	—	—	+ +	—

[a] Acids in wine extracts converted to methyl esters for gas chromatography.

[b] — = no peak discernible; ? = trace peak present, identity by relative retention time only; + to + + + + = relative amounts in extracts, identity by IR.

TABLE 2B (80)

Acids Previously Reported Present in Volatile Extracts of Cabernet Sauvignon Wines

Compound	Identification	
	Method	Date
Formic	PC[a]	1964
Acetic	PC	1964
Propionic	PC	1964
Butyric	GC	1964
Isobutyric	GC, PC	1964
Valeric	GC	1964
Isovaleric	GC, PC	1964
Caproic	GC, PC	1964
Enanthic	GC	1964
Caprylic	GC, PC	1964
Pelargonic	GC	1964
Capric	GC	1964
Lauric	GC	1964
Ethyl acid succinate	GC, IR	1964

[a] PC = paper chromatography, GC = gas chromatography, IR = infrared spectrophotometry.

53

TABLE 3B (80)

Neutral Compounds Reported Present in Volatile Extracts of Cabernet Sauvignon Wines

Compound	Identification Method[a]	Date	Compound	Identification Method[a]	Date
Methanol	GC	1965	Ethyl formate	GC	1965
Ethanol	GC	1964	Ethyl acetate	GC	1964
n-Propanol	GC	1964	Ethyl propionate	GC	1965
2-Butanol	GC	1966	Ethyl isobutyrate	GC	1965
2-Methylpropanol	GC	1964	Ethyl 4-hydroxybutyrate	GC	1966
n-Butanol	GC	1964	Ethyl isovalerate	GC	1967
2-Methylbutanol	GC	1964	Ethyl caproate	GC	1964
3-Methylbutanol	GC	1964	Ethyl caprylate	GC	1964
n-Pentanol	GC	1965	Ethyl caprate	GC	1964
2-Pentanol	GC	1966	Ethyl lactate	GC	1964
n-Hexanol	GC	1964	Ethyl pyruvate	GC	1966
n-Heptanol	GC	1965	Diethyl succinate	GC	1964
2-Phenethanol	GC	1964	Diethyl malate	GC	1966
Farnesol	TL	1966	n-Propyl acetate	GC	1966
Linaloöl	TL	1966	Isobutyl acetate	GC	1964
Methanal	PC	1965	Isobutyl valerate	GC	1967
Ethanal	PC	1965	Isobutyl caproate	GC	1965
Propanal	PC	1965	Isabutyl lactate	GC	1966
Isobutanal	GC	1966	n-Butyl acetate	GC	1966
Isopentanal	PC	1965	Isoamyl acetate	GC	1964
n-Butanal	GC	1966	Isoamyl isovalerate	GC	1965
n-Hexanal	GC	1966	Isoamyl caproate	GC	1964
n-Octanal	PC	1965	Isoamyl caprylate	GC	1964
Furfural	GC	1966	Isoamyl lactate	GC	1964
Cinnamaldehyde	GC	1966	n-Hexyl acetate	GC	1964
Acetone	GC	1966	n-Hexyl caprylate	GC	1964
-Ionone	TL	1966	2-Phenethyl acetate	GC	1964
Acetal	GC	1964	2-Phenethyl caproate	GC	1964
Methyl acetate	GC	1966	-Butyrolactone	GC	1964

[a] GC = gas chromatography, TL = thin layer chromatography, PC = paper chromatography.
[b] References at end of article.

TABLE 4B (80)

Relative Concentrations of Neutral Components in Extracts of Four Cabernet Wines

| | | Cabernet Sauvignon | | | Ruby Cabernet |
| | | 1960, distilled | | 1955 | 1967 |
Peak No.	Component	Wood-aged	Not aged	CH_2CL_2 ext.	CH_2Cl_2 ext.
10	Isobutanol	+ [a]	+	+ + +	+ + +
14	Iso and act. amyl alcs.	+ + + +	+ + + +	+ + + +	+ + + +
15A	Unk., no IR	—	+	—	+ +
16A	3-Methylpentanol	+ +	+	?	?
17	n-Hexanol	+ + +	+ + +	+	+
18	Ethyl lactate	+ + + +	+ + + +	+ + + +	+ + + +
20	Unk., no IR	—	—	—	+ +
24	Ethyl caprylate	+	+ +	+	+
26	Isoamyl caproate	+	+	—	—
29	Ethyl 3-hydroxybutyrate	?	?	+	+
30	Unk., possibly ketone	?	+	?	+
31	Ethyl 2-hydroxyisocaproate	+	+	+	?
32	Unk., IR like ethyl 2-hydroxy-3-methyl-valerate	+ +	+	+ +	+
33	Ethyl 3-hydroxypropionate	—	—	+	—
35	Gamma-Butyrolactone	?	?	+ + +	+ +
36	Ethyl caprate	?	+	?	+
37	Diethyl succinate	+ + + +	+ +	+ + +	+ +
37A	Isoamyl caprylate	?	+	?	?
38	Unk., no IR	?	?	+ +	+
39	Unk., gamma-lactone	—	—	—	+ + +
41	2-Phenethyl acetate	+	+ + +	—	?
45	Benzyl alcohol	+ +	+	+ +	+
46	2-Phenethanol	+ + + +	+ + + +	+ + + +	+ + + +
47	Unk., unsat. alc.	?	?	+	?
48	Unk., gamma-lactone	+	?	+	?
51	Diethyl malate	+	+	+	?
52	Unk., gamma-lactone	?	?	+	?
53	Unk., hydroxy ester + lactone (as in sherry)	?	?	+ +	?
54	p-Ethylphenol	+ +	+	+ +	—
57	4-Carboethoxy-4-hydroxybutyric acid lactone	—	—	+ +	+
58	Ethyl 2-hydroxy-3-phenyl-propionate	+ +	+	+ +	+
60	Diethyl tartrate	+	—	+	—

[a] — = no peak present; ? = small peak present but identification by relative retention times only; + to + + + + = relative amounts of components in extracts with identification by IR.

TABLE 5B (68)

Pigment contents of V. *vinifera* grape varieties, sampled from the Barossa Valley

	Amounts per berry (mg)	
Grape variety	Tannin pigments	Total anthocyanins
Shiraz	2.1	2.6
Cabernet Sauvignon	3.3	3.1
Malbec	2.5	3.7
Grenache	2.6	1.5
Mataro	3.8	3.0
Red Muscat Frontignac	2.2	0.3

TABLE 6B (68)

Colour characteristics and pigment contents of young varietal wines (4–5 months old)

					Pigment content g/l	
Wine variety	max. (nm)	min. (nm)	Colour Density (1 mm cell)	Colour Tint	Tannin Pigments	Total Antho-cyanins
Shiraz (Barossa Valley)	535	430–460	0.73	0.66	1.9	0.91
Shiraz (Murray Valley)	535	430–460	0.54	0.70	0.9	0.40
Cabernet Sauvignon	538	430–450	0.89	0.62	2.4	0.98
Malbec	535	420–440	1.28	0.49	3.2	0.64
Mataro	540	440–460	0.60	0.67	1.5	0.45
Grenache	528	430–460	0.29	0.78	1.2	0.36

APPENDIX X

Pigment profiles of wine
grape varieties sampled from
the Barossa Valley, 1967
season. (Somers)

The numbers of berries used
in the analyses are shown in
brackets.

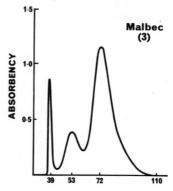

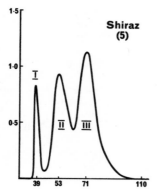

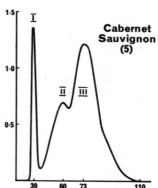

Bibliography

1. Amerine, M. A., Berg, H. W., Cruess, W. V., *Technology of Winemaking*, 3rd Ed. A.V.I. Pub. Co., Westport, Connecticut, 1972

2. Amerine, M. A., Joslyn, M. A., *Table Wine*, 2nd Ed. U.C. Press, California, 1970

3. Amerine, M. A., Joslyn, M. A., *V.C. California Agricultural* Experimental Station Bulletin 639, 1940

4. Amerine, M. A., Winkler, A. J., *California wine grapes, V.C. California Agricultural Experimental Station Bulletin 693*, 1963

5. Antcliff, A. M., *Ampelography & Choice of Varieties, 5th Viticultural Seminar N.S.W. Dpt. Agriculture*, 1976

6. Bayonome, C., Cordonnier, R., Dubois, P., *Etude d'une fraction caracteristique de l'arome du raisin de la variete Cabernet-Sauvignon: mise en evidence de la 2-methoxy-3 -isobutyb-pyrazine. Compt. rend. Acad. Sci. (Paris) 281D:75–78*, 1975

7. Beck, E. James, *Wine: its History, Culture & Making*, Rhine Castle Wines, First Edition Reprint, 1946

8. Benwell, Sam, *Coonawarra a Vignoble*, Mildara/Wilke & Co., Victoria, 1971

9. Bleasdale, Rev. John, *Intercolonial Exhibition 1866–67: Jurors' report on wines*, 1867

10. Bleasdale, Rev. John, *On Colonial Wines*, 1867

11. Bleasdale, Rev. John, *International Exhibition Essays No. 6*, Mason etc. Melbourne, 1872–3

12. Bleasdale, Rev. John, *Present conditions & prospects of the Wine Industry in Australia*, Bailliere, Melbourne, 1876

13. Bleasdale, Rev. John, *Essay on the wines sent to the late intercolonial exhibition*, Bailliere, Melbourne, 1876

14. Boehm, E. W., Tulloch, H. W., *Grape Varieties of South Australia*, Dpt. Agriculture S.A., Adelaide, 1967

15. Boidron, Jean-Noel, *Essai d'Identification des Constituants de l'arome des vins de* Vitis vinifera, Thesis Univ. Bordeaux, 1966

16. Bordeaux Wine Exhibition, *Official Catalogue of the Wines of N.S.W.*, Government Printer, 1882

17. Broadbent, Michael, *Wine Tasting*, 3rd

Ed., Christie Wine Publications, London, 1975

18. Busby, James, a. *Report on the vines, New South Wales*, 1832 b. *Catalogue Botanical Garden*, 1834

19. Cairncross, S. E., Sjöstrom, L. B., *Flavour profiles—a new approach to flavour problems*, Food Technol., 4.308, 1950

20. Cocks, Ch., Feret, Ed., *Bordeaux et ses vins 12/2*, Feret et Fils, Bordeaux, 1974

21. Conference Fruit-Growers, *Vine Growers*, N.S.W. Government Printer, 1890

22. Cosmo, I., Forti, R., Sardi, F., *Cabernet Sauvignon*, Ann. Sper. Agr. 13 Supp. 2, LXXV–LXXXIV.

23. De Castella, Francois. *The Grapes of South Australia*, Phylloxera Board S.A., Adelaide, 1942

24. De Castella, Hubert. *Wine Growing in British Colonies*, Proc. Roy-Colonial Institute Vol. 19, 1887–8

25. Druitt, Robert, *Report on the Cheap wines from . . . and Australia*, 2nd Ed. Henry Renshaw, London, 1873

26. Elliott, John F., *Climatology of the Vine*, W.A. Dept, of Agriculture Review, quotes Prescott, J. A., Gladstones, J. S., Rankine, Bryce, 1972

27. Evans, Len, *Australia and New Zealand Complete Book of Wine*, Sydney, Paul Hamlyn, 1973.

28. Evans, Len, Halliday, James. *The Bulletin*, p.41, Sydney, Dec. 25, 1976.

29. Feret, Edward, *Bordeaux and its wines*, 2nd English Ed., 1883

30. Gagnon, A. J., *Grape Varieties & Soils of the Bordeaux Region*, Wines & Vines, Vol. 54, No. 5 p. 15, 1973

31. Grasby, W. Catton, *Coonawarra Fruit Colony*, Adelaide, 1899

32. Guyot, Jules, *Culture of the Vine & Winemaking*, Walker, May, Melbourne, 1865

33. Hanckel, Norman, *Australia & New Zealand Complete Book of Wine*, p. 466, 1973

34. Jacquelin, Louis, Poulain, Rene, *Vignes et vins de France*, Librarie Flammarion, Paris, 1966

35. Jefferson, Thomas, *Tour notes on wines & vines in France and Italy, 1787*. Vinifera Wine Growers Ass:, Plains, Virginia, 1976

36. Johnston, Moira, *The Year California won the Pennant*, New West, p. 88, Aug., 2, 1976

37. Kahn, J. H., *Compounds identified in whisky, wine, beer*, Journal A.A.C. 52:1166, 1969

38. Kahn, Odette, *A tasting of California wines*, Revue du vin de France, p. 5, No. 260, Nov. 1976

39. Kelly, Alex C., *Wine Growing in Australia*, Wigg, Adelaide, 1867

40. Kelly, Alex C., *The Vine in Australia*, Sands & Kenny, Sydney, 1861

41. Kepner, Richard E., Dinsmoor Webb, A., and Muller, J. Carlos, *Identification of 4-hydroxy 3-methyloctanoic acid gamma-lactone (5-Butyl-4-methyldihydro-2-(3H)-furanone) as a volatile component of oak-wood-aged wines of Vitis Vinifera Var. 'Cabernet Sauvignon'*, Amer, J. Enol. Viticult., Vol. 23 No. 3, 1972

42. Lake, Max, *Claret style in Australia*, Australian Wine Consumers Bulletin, 1(10) Sydney, 1959

43. Lake, Max, *Classic Wines of Australia*, 3rd printing, 1966

44. Lake, Max, *Flavour of wine*, Jacaranda Press, Brisbane, 1969

45. Lake, Max, *Homage to Cabernet Sauvignon* (4 parts), Medical Practice Management 2, (2–5), 1973

46. Lake, Max, *Cabernet Sauvignon in Australia*, Paragon of Wines & Spirits, Vol. 2 Heidelberg Pub. London, 1973

47. Lake, Max, *Cabernet Sauvignon, the exquisite paradox*. J. K. Walker Lecture, 1976.

48. Larousse: *Dictionnaire des Vins*, Paris, 1969

49. McGlothlin, John, Sullivan, Charles L., *California Cabernet Sauvignon*, Wine Magazine 86, p. 33, 1973

50. Moonen, Leo, *Australian Wines*, Watt, Melbourne, 1883

51. Murphy, Dan, *Classification of Australian Wines*, Sun Books, Melbourne, 1974

52. Ordish, George, *The Great Wine Blight*, Bent, London, 1972

53. Peel, Lynette, *Viticulture at Geelong & Lilydale*, Royal Hist. Soc. Victoria vol. 36, Melbourne, 1965

54. Penning-Rowsell, Edmund, *The Wines of Bordeaux*, 3rd Ed., Penguin Books, Middlesex, England, 1973

55. Petit-Lafitte, August, *La Vigne dans le Bordelais*, Paris, 1868

56. Pettavel, David Louis, *A Concise & practical treatise on the Cultivation of the Vine*, Geelong Prize Essay, 1859

57. Peynaud, Emile, *Connaissance et Travail du Vin*, p.70, Dunod, Paris, 1971.

58. *Plant Catalogue in the Royal Society's Gardens*, Hobart Town, Carbenet Savignien, 1857

59. Preece, Colin, *The Dry Red Wines of South East Australia*, A.N.U. Symposium on Australian Wines, 1956

60. Ray, Cyril, *Lafite*, Peter Davies, London, 1968

61. Ray, Cyril, Mouton Rothschild, Christies, London, 1974

62. Seabrook, Doug, *Starting a Cellar*, Epicurean, 66, p. 20, 1977

63. Seabrook, T. C., *Some Observations on Wine*, J. K. Walker Lecture, Wine & Food Society, N.S.W., 1948

64. Simon, André, *Wines, Vineyards and Vignerons of Australia*, Lansdowne, Sydney, 1966

65. Simon, André, *Wines of the World*, McGraw Hill, London, 1967

66. Singleton, Vernon, *Reynell Lecture 'Wine Aging & its Future'*, Roseworthy College, South Australia, 1976

67. Somers, T. C., *In search of quality for red wines*, Food Technol. Australia, 27, p. 49, 1975

68. Somers, T. C., *Pigment profiles of grapes and of wines*, Vitis Band 7, p. 303, 1968

69. Sutcliffe, Serena, *Grapes & their effect on wine II*, J. Internat, Wine & Food Society, Vol. 3, No. 2, p. 19, 1976

70. Sutherland Smith, David, *J. K. Walker Lecture*, Wine & Food Society, N.S.W., 1952

71. Suttor, George, *Culture of the Grape Vine & the Orange in* Australia & New Zealand, Smith Elder, London, 1843

72. Thompson, John F., *Climate, Microclimate & Site Selection Tasmania Journal Agric.* Vol. 47, p. 141, 1976

73. Thorp, John R., *Viticulture in Tasmania, the choice of a grape*, J. Agric. Tasmania, p. 149, Aug. 1976

74. Thorpy, Frank, *New Zealand Wine Guide*, 1976

75. *Thomson's Liquor Guide*, Chippendale, Sydney, 1976

76. Viala, P., Vormerl, V. *Traité Général de Viticulture, Ampelographie*, Vol. 2, p. 285 & p. 6, 1901

77. *Vigneron, The*, Vol. 1, No. 5, p. 55 *Report by Chief Inspector Distilleries N.S.W. (Carbinet Sources & strengths)*, 1886

78. Virzetelly, *Wines of the World*, (Vienna Exhibition fracas), 1888

79. Webb, A. D., *Chemistry & Physiology of Flavours*, A.V.I. Publ. Co., Westport, Connecticut, 1967

80. Webb, A. D., Kepner, R. E., Maggiora, L., *Some volatile components of wines of v. vinifera varieties Cabernet Sauvignon and ruby cabernet*, 1 & 2 Vol. 20, p. 16–31, 1969

81. Whitington, E., *South Australian Vintage*, 'The Register', Adelaide, 1903

82. Winkler, A. J., Olno, H. P., *Cabernet Sauvignon, Wines Wines* 18 (6) 4–5, June 1937

83. Younger, William, *Gods, Man & Wine.* Michael Joseph, London, 1966

Index

Chateaux are listed by name.
The appendices are another index in themselves.